WHAT READERS ARE SAYING...

"Ruben Estrada was, and is, my friend. I say was, because his body has passed. I say is, because his wit, wisdom, and heart remains with us as his gift to the world. Ruben's book, *Know Your Next Move,* is the story of a journey to full consciousness as a player in the game of life. Through Ruben's delightful and deceptively simple telling of the story of growth and development, we all can see ourselves, growing and developing as successful CEOs, managers, and coaches, and contributing members of our economies, communities, and families.

Ruben's true gift was in his Presence and his ability to Empower his friends (and Ruben has thousands of friends) to be great in what they were up to in their lives. This book is more than a business or self-help manual. It is a roadmap and guide for anyone who wants to improve – in business and in life. Do yourself a favor and read *Know Your Next Move.* You will benefit from the experience well beyond the reading."

— John King
   Author – *Tribal Leadership*
   Rogue Scholar – Cultural Architect

D1590760

"Ruben Estrada's gift is to zero in on those strategies that are MUST DO for every business owner, regardless of your business size and longevity, and to explain it in simple terms so that you don't need a PhD to follow along. In fact, because Ruben uses the parable story-telling style, you will be riveted to see what happens next to the business owner in this book – a business owner that could very well be you. As the former co-owner and president of the largest sales and management training company in the world, 44 years in business, I saw myself in the story repeatedly.

I urge you to quickly read the Table of Contents. Words like Systems, Culture, Growth, Client Retention, Administration, and Information Technology will jump off the page and form a simple question in your mind: 'Am I successfully doing these disciplines in my business?'

If you are not 100% confident you and your team are living these core business disciplines every day, I urge you to buy this book for yourself and for every member of your management team. Read the book together. Discuss it together. And together, you will begin to understand the strategies that are paramount for every business owner. Then, contact an Estrada Strategies Coach to hold you accountable and stretch your comfort zone."

— Bruce Seidman
   Former President / Owner
   Sandler Systems, Inc.

KNOW YOUR NEXT MOVE

A Parable on
The 7 Core Disciplines
of Business

RUBEN A. ESTRADA

Estrada Family Trust

Know Your Next Move
A Parable on the 7 Core Disciplines of Business

Published by
Estrada Family Trust
San Bernardino, California
www.EstradaStrategies.com/Ontario

Copyright © 2013 *by Ruben Estrada*
Cover Design by Dan Mulhern Design
Interior Design by Dawn Teagarden

ISBN: 978-0-9892757-0-5

Printed in the United States of America
www.estradastrategies.com /ontario

This book is dedicated to you...
the Reader, the Entrepreneur, the Business Owner.

My purpose in life has been to support your success as you are
the backbone of our economy, and I pray that this book brings
you tips, strategies, systems, and ideas that you can apply in
your business to make it sustainable and successful.

CONTENTS

Dear Reader,

Most of the small to mid-sized business owners I meet have successfully grown businesses that provide quality services and products. Yet when they cross my path, they are at a crossroad for one reason or another. They have done very well, and are basically stable, but their future growth is limited by their lack of business acumen (problem-solving, research, study and learning, and business skills). Others have really gone beyond their initial expectations, achieved great things in their business, and simply do not know where to go next. And then there are some truly on the verge of collapse — if not in the business, in their personal life. The business has either grown beyond their current capacity, or it's ready to implode for lack of systems and processes, and the impact of the stress can be seen everywhere.

All of these entrepreneurs know that there are areas where they can increase efficiency, productivity, and profitability, but they are not quite sure where to start. They have trouble identifying their next move, and the ones on the verge of collapse know they need help quickly. They've poured just about every resource they have — their time, their energy, their money, etc. — into keeping the business above water, but they are not getting the results. Many of them have broken promises to their loved ones because they are the only ones who can handle the crisis, and are suffering the disconnection with their families. Several are beginning to feel the impact on their health, and know they need help before they lose it all.

Why does this happen?

Well, people can still grow an impressive business, but when push comes to shove and they do not have the knowledge and skills to manage and grow the business, or a personal emergency takes their focus away from the business, they fall apart. And when they do, families are broken apart, marriages are shattered, and lives are destroyed.

If you can relate to being at a crossroad in your business, and you know you don't know what you don't know, you have picked up the right book.

Many years ago, I began teaching business owners *The 7 Core Disciplines of Business* — disciplines that, when mastered, allow a CEO to grow a phenomenally successful business without sacrificing their sanity, their family, and their health. The result of understanding and implementing these disciplines is predictable growth, success, and freedom. I've seen it over and over again, and now I want to make it available to the masses.

I wrote *Know Your Next Move* as a parable to make it easy for business owners at any stage of business development to learn (or deepen their understanding of) *The 7 Core Disciplines of Business* and begin to identify the gaps that are causing them the most pain. You will take the journey — cognitively and emotionally — with the main character, as he engages these disciplines systematically for the first time with the help of a Coach like me.

I know, like the main character, you will feel a myriad of emotions and have lots of questions arise as you work through this process, and I want to encourage you to read this with a journal nearby so that you can record all of your AHAs, insights, and questions as you go. In fact, I have inserted this symbol where I know you will likely need a moment to pause and take notes.

Now, implementing the Disciplines into your business will require another level of support because every business and every CEO are different. As you read the story, consider what it would be like to have your own Coach working with you to identify your next move, grow your business beyond its current limits and, maybe even more importantly, allow you to relax, knowing that if you had to step away from the business — for a family vacation, for a personal crisis, or for the sale of the business — everything would continue on seamlessly without you.

Can you imagine that type of growth and freedom — to live life and lead your business on your terms?

I know and believe it is possible for you because I have helped hundreds of business owners, and because I am living proof of the power of this message.

These disciplines gave *me* the room to grow and experience that freedom, and to be the husband, father, leader, and mentor I have always wanted to be. They also gave me the opportunity to save my own life when the biggest test of the disciplines appeared two years ago and forced me to step away from the business. Instead of collapsing, the company grew in my absence, and I was able to take some time to write down the lessons that made it all possible.

May your CEO journey be blessed with wild success,

You Don't Know What You Don't Know

"We grow and mature as leaders faster when sitting at the edge of our comfort zone than when resting in the center."

~ Coach ~

Why is this happening? What went wrong?

I asked myself the same questions over and over, hoping that the answers would magically appear.

Four years of steady growth, and now it's unraveling?

I sank into my seat and closed my eyes, trying to steady myself for the task ahead. My heart had been racing at a terrifying pace for almost eight months now, and the pains in my chest were beginning to worry me. Exhaustion and fear were taking their toll.

Pull yourself together, Ruben. Breathe, man. The answers to all of your questions are out there.

Pull yourself together, Ruben. Breathe, man. The answers to all of your questions are out there.

The faces of the employees who had been critical to our growth drifted across the back of my eyelids, and I found myself searching their expressions for the reasons for their departures, the decline in morale, and the downward spiral that was my business. I searched and searched, but still, no answers.

What am I going to do? How long can I continue to personally fund this business and put in these hours before everything crumbles? I need help.

I had hired a team of consultants to come in and assess my business at the bargain price of $100,000. It took two months to complete and when it was all said and done, I was left with three 3-inch binders full of information about my business that I already knew. One binder had six pages of suggested action items with a ridiculous price for the consulting firm to help me implement each item. The pain of wasting two months and $100K (and being taken for a ride by this firm) was almost too much.

And how long is my family going to hang in there with me?

I was working twelve-hour days, seven days a week, and my family was suffering. I was missing time with them, and my wife was beginning to feel neglected in addition to very concerned about our financial future. I was burning out, in foreign territory, and running out of options. Just when I thought it could not get worse, our largest and oldest customer called and insisted that I, not one of my reps, fly out to visit with them if we wanted to keep their account.

"What do you mean you are going to Dallas to visit a customer?" My wife's voice had been tense with anger and exhaustion. "Your son has a play at school, and you promised him you would attend. He will be very disappointed and so will I." The disappointment in her beautiful brown eyes made me catch my breath before answering.

"You don't understand, this is our largest client, and if I don't go to visit him, he will quit service, and we just can't afford that." Our relationship had gone beyond understanding each other and entered a phase of arguing about every decision I made.

How can I make her understand? I'm doing this for us.

The tension between us was so thick that I found myself withdrawing, hoping that I could just keep my head about me enough to turn the business around…and then I would have more time at home.

I have to save this customer. I have to find a solution.

I remember sitting on the plane, with my eyes closed, knowing that there had to be a solution. *Praying* for a solution was more like it.

It was a long flight from California to Dallas, Texas, and the plane was full. I had planned on taking advantage of the flight time to pore through mail, and write emails to my managers, giving them detailed instructions on what needed to be handled while I was away. You know, the important stuff a CEO must do to keep the doors open. Yet, I also knew that every person I met was a potential customer and had made it a habit to strike up a conversation with anyone willing to talk.

"How are you doing?" I asked the man sitting next to me. He looked to be in his fifties, healthy, clean cut, powerful, and yet unassuming.

"I'm doing beeeaaauuutifully." He strung the word out as if he really meant it. He seemed warm and sincere. Curious as to his profession, I imagined him as the CEO of a large company or a very polished and successful politician. Either one could be a prospect for my services. Knowing that, in sales, if you can get someone to talk about themselves, you can get them to talk about anything, I looked for a way to begin a real conversation.

On his seat tray was a note pad with only the words "Begin with the End in Mind" written on it.

Perfect.

"I can't help but notice what you wrote on your pad. What does that mean to you?" I asked.

"Do you own or run a business, young man?"

> *"Can your company run without you for, let's say, a six-month period?"*

"Yes, I do. I own a company in California that has been in business for four years, and we have been growing at a rate of 21% each year," I proudly answered.

"Can your company run without you for, let's say, a six-month period?"

I was taken back by his question, but something about the way he asked the question made me want to answer honestly.

"Well, to be honest, no. If I were to step out for an extended period of time, I think the business may collapse."

After answering his question, I felt a bit vulnerable and somewhat uncomfortable.

Who is this guy I just started to spill my guts out to? Did I just open myself up for a sales pitch? What if he was another one of those "consulting firms" that promises to come in and fix all your problems?

"Don't feel bad. You are not alone. In my experience, more than 90% of small business owners, of businesses that generate less than $50 million in sales, have not 'Begun with the End in Mind.' Many of them continue to do very well with their business anyway."

Okay, no sales pitch. No solution. No "let me tell you..." response.

He just sat there, looking at me with a curious and comforting expression. Something told me that this person was full of knowledge and wisdom, and I wanted to hear more.

"Okay, you got my curiosity. What does 'Begin with the End in Mind' mean to a guy like me who owns a fast-growing, $6 million dollar a year company?"

"What is your name, young man?"

"My name is Ruben." I extended my hand to shake his. "And you are...?"

His handshake was strong and confident, further adding to my liking of him.

"Most people just call me Coach. Ruben, I will answer your question, but I must also tell you that I am always coaching. That is my life, and I know nothing else. What that means is that I may ask you questions in this brief conversation that are uncomfortable for you to answer. I want you to know this because I firmly believe that we grow and mature as leaders faster when sitting at the edge of our comfort zone than when resting in the center. Much of what I do is designed to put you on that edge, and then I will help you to expand your comfort zone by adding my experiences and knowledge to yours. Also, please keep in mind that we are just having a conversation. I have no intention of trying to sell you anything. So, do you still want me to answer your question?"

At the end of the day, when you move to transition out of your business by selling it, franchising it, taking it public, or transitioning it to the next generation, your businesses is worth more when it can operate without you, than if you are needed to run it.'

Wow, now this guy has really got my attention. In all my years in business, I have never come across someone with a line like that.

I made a mental note to write that one down and use it one day on a prospect.

"Yes, if you ask me something I am uncomfortable answering, I will tell you and may not give you an answer," I replied, trying to compete intellectually for control.

"Fair enough. It is obvious to me you like to be in control of conversations and, in fact, coaching works much better that way. So let's circle back to your question."

What? Can this guy read my mind, or is he really that good?

"So Ruben, 'Beginning with the End in Mind' speaks to one rule in business. That rule reads 'At the end of the day, when you move to transition out of your business by selling it, franchising it, taking it public, or transitioning it to the next generation, your business is worth more when it can operate without you, than if you are needed to run it.' What does that rule mean to you?"

I quickly got a blank note pad out to write what he just said.

There was something else he said that I wanted to write down. What was that?

Formulating my answer to his question seemed to have crowded out his words.

"Right now, it means that I am never going to sell my business!" I spat back with a bit more edge than I intended. His statement made so much sense and yet, after twenty years in business as a leader, and four years with my own company, no one had ever put it quite that way before.

"I have never heard that rule, put in that way, so clearly. But how do I get my business to run without me? I just can't see it happening any time soon." I was starting to feel frustrated with the question because I did not know the answer. "Oh, and can you repeat that rule? I want to write it down correctly."

"Sure, but why don't we share your note pad? I will put my notes in it as we talk, and when we are done, you will have all my tips in your journal for future reference. This is your journal, correct?" He offered.

"No, it's not a journal, just a note pad I picked up on the way out. But I like your idea of sharing it."

"Do you keep a journal?"

"No." I could feel the sweat beginning to bead on my brow.

Keep a journal? For what?

As if hearing my thoughts, he continued, "Where do you keep a repository of all the short-term and long-term initiatives you and your team are working towards?"

"I don't." The moment I answered the question, I felt on the edge of that comfort zone he had described.

"Should you?" His eyes and the edges of his lips turned up, as if he were suppressing a smile.

Damn this guy. He keeps asking questions that I don't like!

"I guess I should," was all I could answer. I felt like a high school kid explaining to the teacher why I did not do my homework.

"If you did, what value would it bring you as a CEO? What value would it bring the managers who report to you? And what would the journal look like?" Before I could answer, he continued. "Would you be the only executive keeping a journal, or would you require all mangers to journal with their department employees?"

STOP ALREADY!

My mind screamed, trying to keep up with him, while my frustration over not having the answers started to make my heart race.

As a CEO, 50% of your time is spent delegating with follow-up. It's all about getting results from others. You need a system to do that.

"You don't have to answer these questions right now. I will, however, ask that you write them down in your new journal and make a commitment to find the answers. I will repeat the questions so you can write them down." He repeated them and waited for me to finish taking the notes.

"Now, as it relates to creating a journaling system for your company:

1. **What** are you going to do?
2. **When** are you going to do it?
3. **How** am I going to know you got it done?

Those are the three most impactful questions you will ask of your people every time you delegate a new initiative to them. Keep in mind that, as a CEO, 50% of your time is spent delegating with follow-up. It's all about getting results from others. You need a system to do that. So, Ruben, how are you going to answer my three questions of you?

I was amazed. I had only been talking with Coach for thirty minutes and had filled three pages with notes. I felt like I had learned more about leadership and what a CEO should be focusing on in the last thirty minutes than in my last twenty years in business. I wanted, no, I needed, more.

"Well?" Coach's eyes were as eager as his question.

I took a deep breath, feeling the pressure of getting this first assignment right. "Okay. Question 1: What am I going to do? I am going to:

- identify the value that keeping a journal of delegated initiatives would bring me as the CEO,

- ask my managers to do the same for their positions after I review this concept with them,

- draft out what a journal would look like, using these three questions as a guideline,

- and finally, I will begin using the journal with my managers first, for ninety days before requiring them to implement it with their employees in their departments.

"Question 2: When am I going to do it? I will:

- have the value list done by the end of the week,

- meet with the managers next week and have their list by the following Friday,

- complete the draft of the journal by that same Friday, and

- launch this initiative the following Monday."

Just taking the time to think through this initiative was invigorating and exciting. I could see so many of my issues and concerns about what my managers are doing going away with this system.

We would all be on the same page!

"Question 3: How are you going to know I got this done? Well, I will have to email you my plan and send you an update with each milestone date. Will that work for you?"

He handed me his business card. "Outstanding. I am impressed with your ability to quickly develop a plan of action. I agree with all of your steps and feel you can meet those target dates. Feel free to call me as well, should you get stuck along the way." He paused and looked intently at me. "One more question, what do you want me to do if you don't send the email updates?"

Crap! He got me again. This guy is all about accountability! But he is letting me define all the steps, even those leading up to consequences. Interesting...

"Well, that won't happen. If I say I am going to do something by a certain date, it gets done!" I answered with my head held high.

"Is that also true for all your managers?" Coach asked, and then quickly added, "Don't answer. Think."

"I don't know that I can think anymore. You have my head spinning with new opportunities. I want to learn more. Tell me, how does your coaching program work?" I had to ask. There was something really special about this guy. As much as he had just pushed me out of my comfort zone, I appreciated the way he had done it. He had just given me hugely valuable lessons, by asking me questions, and had not even begun to tell me about his program. His approach was completely different than the other consultants I had engaged.

"Ruben, I made a promise to you that I would not try to sell you anything during this conversation, and I never break my promises. I will tell you that to become a client requires a two-hour conversation in which you will have to be qualified. Not every business owner qualifies for our programs. Also, I must be clear that I am not a consultant, and I will not do the work for you. No, I am a coach, which means you will have to do the work, and I will coach you through it. Before that, let's see how you do with this journal initiative; this will be part of the qualification process."

"Thank you, Coach, I won't let you down." For some reason, I wanted to impress this guy more than I had wanted to impress anyone else.

And I love a good challenge.

"I know you won't because this is not about me; it is about you, and you won't let yourself down." The flight attendant announced landing instructions. Somehow, almost three hours had sped by in a flash.

I began to wonder what it would be like to have a CEO Coach on my team. I had so many questions for him, but we had run out of time. For the first time in four years, I was beginning to see what the end could look like if I got the right guidance and did the work.

I haven't been this excited about my business in a while.

"Another thing, Ruben, before we part ways: you are going to have a lot of questions for me. Please write them in your journal under a page with my name on it, and we can discuss them when you call. Talk to you soon." He shook my hand again before he turned to walk away.

"Coach, one more question before you leave. If you could put into one word the key to having a business that runs with out me, what would that word be?"

"Systems, Ruben. Systems. There are seven Disciplines of business that must be systematized for any business to be fully sustainable and replicable. They are called the Core Disciplines of Business, and we will review them in our next conversation. For now, you have plenty to work on over the next thirty days." Coach abruptly turned and walked away, and then he stopped and strode back toward me. "One more thought, Ruben. In business *you don't know what you don't know,* and it is what you don't know that *will* get in your way."

I quickly wrote that one down with all of the other notes.

As I watched Coach leave the gate, I realized that I knew very little about him. On his business card, there was no title. Only the name of his business, with an interesting slogan "Your Next Move" with six chess pieces as their logo.

I need someone to show me how to save this business before it costs me the rest of my life.

Thanks to him, I know my next move is to get this journal thing down and then do whatever I have to do to qualify as one of his clients. I need this type of accountability. I need someone to show me how to save this business before it costs me the rest of my life.

As I walked through the gate, I knew that no matter what happened with this customer I was going to visit, I was going to be okay.

THE POWER OF SYSTEMS

*"You can not delegate anything
that is not 'systematized,'
and if you cannot delegate it,
then who has to do it?"*

~ Coach ~

Should I call him?

It had been two full weeks, and I had completed everything on my journal assignment.

What if he does not take my call or, worse yet, says he is not interested in working with me? I sent him the email as promised, and his replies were encouraging but brief.

I could not believe that I was having such a hard time picking up the phone to call Coach.

Come on Ruben, you are acting like a high school kid calling a girl. Okay, I am going to call him. If he takes my call, or not, it will be okay. I can always look for a local coach to work with. But Coach was so easy to talk to.

The minute Coach answered the phone, I knew everything was okay. "Hi Ruben, thank you for calling me today. I was beginning to wonder if you were going to call at all. I got your email and was anxious to learn how the coaching journal concept was received by your leadership team."

"Well, to be honest with you, I was a bit uncomfortable making the call. To be really honest, I was afraid you would not take it."

I can't believe I just admitted that.

"Why is that?"

"Coach, I have never had a conversation with someone like you before, and for some reason, I do not feel worthy of your time."

Wow. I don't feel worthy? Did I just say that?

"If I am unwilling or unable to work with you, I will tell you. Listen, I have a phone conference in five minutes. Why don't we schedule a time to talk where we can dedicate a few hours? In that conversation, we will review your coaching journal project, assess your business against the Core Disciplines of Business, and then determine if we want to work together. I must tell you again that when reviewing the Core Disciplines of Business, you will be put on the edge of your comfort zone. Are you ready to have that conversation?"

Thrilled to hear that he was willing to spend more time with me, I answered, "Coach, I am ready when you are."

By the time I had returned from Dallas, the condition of my company had worsened. We lost a few more clients, someone had started a rumor of us closing the doors which caused the employees to become concerned for their jobs, and the bank had called an emergency meeting based on my last month's financials. My wife was upset with me and my boy was very sad that I had missed his performance at school. *If ever there was a time for change, it is now.*

"Let's plan on talking again today at 3:00."

When we got off the phone, I felt a sense of relief.

Promptly at 3:00 p.m., I picked up the phone and called Coach as scheduled. I had cleared my calendar for the remainder of the day, as I was not sure if this meeting would run longer than the scheduled two hours.

"Okay, Ruben. Before we get started, let's lay some ground rules. First, if ever you feel like I am going too deep with my questioning, please tell me. Otherwise, I will not know. Second, I need you to be completely honest with me. Finally, my son has a baseball game at 5:30 that I will not miss, so this conversation will end promptly at 5:00, even if we are not finished. We can always schedule another meeting to finish. Are you okay with these rules?"

Ha!

I had to laugh to myself. Here I was, willing to work until late into the evening if needed, only to learn that Coach has a family commitment that he will not break.

Man, do I have a lot to learn from this guy.

I sent a quick text to my wife "I will be home by 5:30. Tell Junior we are going to the park. Love you."

> *Okay, Ruben. Before we get started, let's lay some ground rules.*

"Sure, I am completely okay with those rules."
I was more than okay. I was excited about having rules of communication.

"Then let's get started." Coach sounded pleased.

First, we reviewed my progress with the coaching journals. I explained how already, after only two weeks, the management team and I were on the same page. I had no doubts about what they were working on, and they were very clear about my expectations.

"All initiatives are documented with start dates and end dates and prioritized as such," I finished, with no attempt to hide my excitement.

"Good job. It sounds like you are off to a good start with the coaching of your leadership team. One question before we move on to the Core Disciplines. Have you scheduled regular coaching sessions with all of your direct reports?"

My heart skipped a beat.

Great question — one that I should have thought of.

"Actually, no. I guess I should."

"Why do you think that is important?"

Here he goes again with those questions.

I wondered if he could tell over the phone that I had already started to squirm in my seat. "It will ensure that we stay on track with their initiatives and give us a regular time to talk one-on-one." I prayed that I answered this one correctly.

"Exactly right. So, when will you have them scheduled, and how will I know it got done?"

Already, I was beginning to pick up on his pattern of coaching. Everything that I agreed to complete would require some sort of completion date and communication of completion.

I can only dream of the day when all my managers operate at that level, and I no longer have to chase down updates on things I had delegated.

"I put this on my journal as an initiative to complete by the end of next week, and I will email you the coaching schedule when it is completed."

"Perfect. Now, let's discuss the Core Disciplines of Business. Are you looking at the document I emailed you?"

"Yes, I am." I was looking at a document that appeared to be an Organizational Chart, but in place of people or titles, there were areas of business focus.

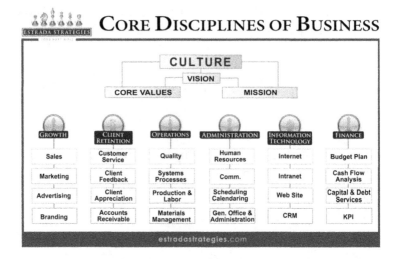

"Great! The chart you are looking at has seven Core Disciplines, and each Discipline has elements below it. What we are going to do is quickly assess how well your company has developed systems for each of these elements. Remember that we have less than two hours to do this, so we must stay at the 30,000-foot level. You will rate your company on a scale of 1 — 5, with a 5 representing a well-systematized element and a 1 representing no systems. Are you with me?"

"Sure. Yet, looking at some of these, I may be at a negative 5. Is that possible?" I was looking at the elements and realizing for the first time that I had no systems in some key areas of business. In fact, there were elements on this chart that I knew nothing about.

What is this Client Appreciation thing all about?

"Funny, but we will stick to a 1 as the lowest rating we can give. Let's get started. To begin, let's make sure we are using the same definition for the word 'Systems.' So tell me, what does it mean to you to have a system for something?"

Finally, a question that I can easily answer.

"Well, a system is something that is documented and happens without much conscious thought."

"Perfect. Remember this rule, 'You cannot delegate anything that is not systematized,' and if you cannot delegate it, then who has to do it?"

You cannot delegate anything that is not systematized.

"Me, I guess."

Did he send someone to spy on my business?

"Correct! I remember a mentor I once had who would ask me the same questions every time he came to my office:

'What are you doing?' And I would tell him what I was doing.

Then he would ask me, 'Why are YOU doing it?' and I would make up some excuse about me being the only person in the organization who knew how to do it.

Then he would challenge me by asking, 'Who do you have in your organization that can do it for you, and what will it take to write a system for it?'

"I learned early in management the power of systems. I learned that well-documented systems can bring all kinds of benefits to the organization. They can be used for training, performance evaluations, the monitoring of the business, and so much more.

When you think of a company with good systems, I want you to think *McDonalds*. They have systems for everything in the business — from how to wash down the parking lot to how food is inventoried and managed. I know because I worked at a *McDonalds* for two years as a kid. So as we discuss each element, and I ask you to rate yourself, you will be rating how well you have developed a system for that element. Got it?"

"Got it."

Is everything this guy says a lesson learned?

My note page was already beginning to fill up, and we had not even really started.

THE FIRST DISCIPLINE
CULTURE

"Culture is the foundation on which the business stands…"

~ Coach ~

We continued to discuss the power of systems for a few minutes longer, and when we were done, I had this amazing image of my company with systems documents for all operational processes. In fact, I had visions of operations manuals for every department in the company. From Sales to Production, everything we did to run this business would be in those manuals.

WOW! I am getting excited.

"Ruben, remember when we were on the airplane and I said, 'You don't know what you don't know'?"

"Yes, I wrote that one down. In fact, I have repeated that saying to everyone over the past few weeks. It makes so much sense." And it really did. I had started taking inventory of what I did well and in which areas of my business I had very little or no knowledge.

My website is contracted out, I am not really close to my financial reports, and I don't even know if our IT department is producing all that it can. And that is only the tip of the iceberg!

"I am glad that CEO Rule was of interest to you. We know that the majority of business owners have never been properly trained in business. For that reason, costly mistakes are made due to a lack of business acumen. Part of my Mission is to increase the business acumen of our clients by offering training and monitoring side-by-side with coaching. Are you with me?"

"Yes, I am very much with you." As Coach had been talking, memories of all the expensive mistakes I have made over the years came flooding back to mind. Things like purchasing a $60,000 accounting software that we never figured out how to use and eventually abandoned, paying $20,000 for a website that we completely changed in less than a year, bad hiring decisions, and excessive compensation to employees who left me high and dry, and so on, and so on.

Yeah, I am with him alright!

I feel like I've been buried under the business, so 30,000 feet sounds like a place where I can take a breath.

"Great. I am telling you all of this because in this conversation, I may have to do some quick training, in addition to coaching, to ensure that you fully understand the Discipline or element we are discussing. Are you okay with that?"

"Absolutely!"

What, are you kidding? You just asked me if I was okay with being trained in key areas of business where I have no knowledge. That's like asking a kid if it is okay to give him a chocolate ice cream while he is taking a pop quiz at school.

"Good, so let's begin. Remember, we are going to stay at 30,000 feet."

"I'm good with that." I eagerly replied.

I feel like I've been buried under the business, so 30,000 feet sounds like a place where I can take a breath.

"Can you tell me what you think about when you think of Culture?" Coach asked.

"Well, when I think of Culture, I think of one's background or where they came from. I am not sure how that applies to a company, but I guess it is about the same." I was not really impressed with my answer.

Sounds like the answer I got from my eight-year-old boy when I found him taking his bike apart. "Well, Dad, I just, kind of, wanted to see how the bike was made." Yeah, that makes sense.

"You have the traditional definition of Culture down. Here is what Culture means to a business. First of all, every business has a Culture, which is either defined by the leadership of the company, or by its employees, customers, vendors, etc. Which do you prefer for your company?"

"Obviously, *I* want to define the Culture for my business." As I said the words, I saw the trap I had walked into.

This is going to hurt…bad!

I could hear Coach take a deep breath on the other end of the phone.

Here it comes. He is going to ask me about my company Culture.

"Good, I was hoping you would answer that way. Now, I am not going to ask you to tell me how you have defined *your* company Culture, as that would not be fair. I will tell you that 98% of the businesses I have coached had no defined Culture when I first met them. So, if that is you, then you are not alone."

Culture is the personality of the business — its character.

Has Coach worked with so many business owners that he has defined our patterned weaknesses? Am I that predictable? How else could he know what I was thinking?

"Here is another CEO Rule for you to remember, 'Culture is a slow turning ship in a large body of water.' That means that changing an organization's Culture takes time. In many cases, changing personnel accompanies the defining of Culture, as some employees simply will not conform. You see, Culture is the personality of the business — its character. Think of culture as the non-knowledge-based skills of the organization. Culture is not industry or product specific, nor is it the same from one company to the next. Yet, every organization has a culture, and it often mirrors the characteristics of its leadership."

The characteristics of my leadership…

Before I could go too far down that rabbit trail, Coach's voice broke into my thoughts again.

"A good friend of mine, John King, coauthored a book titled *Tribal Leadership,* and in it, he makes this statement, 'In business, as in life, Culture eats Strategy for breakfast.'" He paused, allowing that truth to soak in. "I have seen many companies struggle and implode due to a void in Culture. In our world, the Discipline of Culture is comprised of three well-defined elements, and those elements are Vision, Core Values, and Mission. Many people get Vision and Mission mixed up and don't quite understand the difference between them, so I will clear that up now, and when we go to evaluate your business against each element, you will have a basic understanding of each element. Are you following me?"

"Yes, Yes." I took a deep breath.

I am glad he asked me a question. I needed a breath.

My head was spinning. Coach was throwing so much new information at me and I was having a difficult time writing it all down. I wanted to scream SLOW DOWN!

"Okay, cool."

Did he just say "cool"? How can this guy be such a genius and so normal at the same time?

"Vision is that seemingly unrealistic goal that everyone in the organization is striving to achieve, whereas an organization's Mission defines the Strategic Direction for that organization. You with me?"

> *"Vision is that seemingly unrealistic goal that everyone in the organization is striving to achieve, whereas an organization's Mission defines the Strategic Direction for that organization.*

"Yes. The Vision is where we are going and the Mission is how we are going to get there."

"EXACTLY!" I thought I heard a hint of pride in his voice. "You are really getting this."

I bet you say that to all the guys, I thought to myself, even though it did feel good to be praised.

"Core Values, on the other hand, define how you treat the human element along the way. Do you remember the story of Christopher Columbus?"

"Sure."

But please don't ask me to tell the story. I may get it wrong.

"He had the Vision of finding a new route to Asia. He had a defined number of boats, crew, supplies, food, and water to accommodate the estimated time at sea. That was his Mission, or strategy. And, although I do not know if it was ever documented, I have to believe he had some 'rules of conduct' for all of the men who would be sleeping, eating, and working together in close quarters for a long period of time. Those would have been his Core Values. Get it?"

"Got it."

"Good, now tell me what you have learned so far," Coach prompted.

Taking a deep breath to quiet my nerves, I responded, "I learned what company Culture really is, and what elements make up a Culture. I have learned the importance of it and, most importantly, I have realized what a poor job I have done in regards to building it in my company."

Could this have been the reason I lost so many key employees this last year? When we were first starting out, we would get together in my kitchen and talk about the potential of the business and where we wanted to go with it. Today, I cannot remember the last time I had a conversation with my leaders about our future goals and dreams. Could it be that these valuable and key employees who helped build my business simply did not see where we were going any longer? Could it be that I treated them differently with compensation, benefits, bonuses, and responsibility in the business? Could it be that they felt they were not part of defining our strategic direction and, as a result, lost their passion for the business?

> *Could this have been the reason I lost so many key employees this last year?*

Suddenly, I deeply understood the impact Culture has on a business and its employees, customers, vendors, and the community it serves.

As if to relieve some pressure, I moved the phone receiver to my other ear and waited for Coach's response.

"Good lessons you have learned, young Jedi. And to think, we have not even started the systems evaluation process yet. Speaking of that, my clock shows us at 3:45. That leaves us one hour and fifteen minutes. We had better get started because my boy gets real angry if I am late to his games. Ready?"

"Let's roll." I took another deep breath. The truth was that I would have been totally cool to stop here and spend the rest of our time together learning more about Culture, but I also wanted to make sure we got through everything on the agenda for the call.

So much to learn!

"So tell me about your system for your corporate Vision and how you would rate it on a scale of 1-5? Be sure to write your rating next to the element on your Core Disciplines of Business chart."

First one out of the gate, and he got me. Let's see if I can trick him.

"Well, Coach, I do have a Vision for our company, and I would say that most of our employees know what that Vision is, but it is not written down anywhere. So I would give myself about a 4 on that one."

"Can you tell me what that Vision is?"

"Yeah, we want to reach $10 million in sales within the next three years," I proudly and quickly answered.

"That is an excellent goal to have, Ruben. Tell me, what happens if you reach that goal. What happens to your Vision?"

"Well, I guess we will set a new goal." Suddenly, I felt doubtful about how I answered this question.

"Exactly, so let me briefly explain the difference between a Vision and a Goal. Remember when I said that a Vision is a seemingly unrealistic goal that the entire organization is striving to achieve?"

"Yes."

Where is he going with this?

"Well, with a stated annual growth of 22% and a current base of $6 million, is reaching $10 million in three years really a 'seemingly unrealistic' goal?"

He got me.

"Well, not really. In fact, I just signed a five-year contract with a new client that will get us there in two."

"Also, when you defined a system for me early on in our conversation, I believe you said it must be written down. Is that correct?"

Got me again!

"Yeah, that is part of my definition."

"So, if a Vision is a 'seemingly unrealistic' goal and must be written down, then how would you change your rating, on a scale of 1-5, with 5 being well-defined as a system?"

"Remember that comment about a negative number? I think I just found one. I would rate us at a -3." I felt myself squirming and grateful that this interaction was not face-to-face.

And we are still on the first of twenty-seven elements?

Listen Ruben, I hear a little edge in your voice, and that tells me you are moving from the center of your comfort zone.

I almost wanted to ask Coach to stop and help me with Vision before we assessed the other elements.

"Listen Ruben, I hear a little edge in your voice, and that tells me you are moving from the center of your comfort zone. That is okay. If you want to get angry, get angry. If you want to express that frustration with me, go for it. I can take it. In my experience, that is a good sign, as it tells me you are 'getting it,' and are more likely to take action than someone who does not react emotionally. I know that part of you may not want to continue with this exercise in fear that this pattern of no systems will repeat itself over and over again. So what if it does? At least you will know where you stand and will have a road map for improvement. Remember, Ruben, you are *not* the first business owner I have done this with *and* very few have a bunch of 5's when we are done. Are you okay?"

"Yeah, I am okay, but you are right about me being angry. My anger is more around why it took me so long to find someone like you. Where were you two years ago?"

Why do I feel like taking my frustration out on Coach? It's not his fault I didn't find him two years ago.

"Ruben, there are no chances or coincidences in life, only opportunities. Some we see and capitalize on, while others sail right under our noses in plain sight. You and I met on an airplane, you asked me a question, and here we are today. You capitalized on the opportunity in front of you and will be better for it. You cannot change the past, so why waste valuable energy on it? But you can significantly impact the future. That is where I want you to place all your energy from today going forward — the future. Shall we continue?"

"Yeah. Thanks for that, Coach. I do feel a bit better."

But still, where would I be right now if I had met him two years ago? It's going to be hard to let that go.

"Great, now let's get back to the Vision. Here is one you may know: Henry Ford saw a day when the common man could afford a motorized vehicle when, at the time, only the government and the very wealthy had vehicles. Another good example is Dr. Martin Luther King's Vision: He had a dream that one day people would be judged not by the color of their skin but by the content of their character. Millions of people today rally around his Vision."

I think I see what he's saying. My Vision is too small for people to rally behind?

"You see, the purpose of a Vision is to give people a sense of long-term direction, impact, and purpose. A well-written Vision statement will bring passion into the workplace, and I believe people work harder for a passion than they do for a paycheck. In my company, our Vision is "To create an opportunity for all businesses to succeed." Will we ever reach that Vision? In all businesses worldwide? Some say "no," but we believe we will. Everything we do is to serve that Vision and, as a result, our team has developed some amazing programs. Does Coke have a Vision statement? Do Nike and Pepsi? The answer is yes. All Fortune 100 companies have a clear Vision that unites all employees, investors, and even their vendors towards one common goal."

He paused, it seemed, to give me a minute to process what he had just said and catch up before moving on.

"Now, with that new insight on what a Vision is, can I ask you to share your thoughts?"

Here goes…

"First of all, no one has ever explained to me what a Vision Statement is before today. And I can see that if I had a clear Vision Statement written down, everyone in my company would clearly know where we are going and what impact we will have on our industry. I am already thinking of a new Vision. Tell me how this sounds: 'To become the industry's leading innovator, and to set a new standard for quality measurements.'"

"That sounds like a good start, Ruben. If I were to ask you to tell me the story behind that Vision Statement, how would you answer that?"

"What do you mean by story?" My head had started to pound.

A story? What story? I was feeling tripped up again.

"Let me ask the same question a different way. What was the story behind Dr. King's dream?"

"Civil Rights. During his time, there was no equality for people of color. They were treated terribly, and he aimed to change that." I was surprised at how passionate my answer was.

"Now tell me what you think is the story behind our Vision, 'To create an opportunity for all businesses to succeed?'"

"Well, based on the little I know about you and your company, I assume your story has something to do with helping small business owners to get better at running their businesses."

"You are spot on. Our story is founded in the horrific statistics of small business failure and the major contributors to that failure. The #2 reason why businesses fail, according to the 2000

U.S. Census, is a lack of business acumen. According to that census, only 22% of entrepreneurs have a bachelor's degree, and only 11% of Hispanic or Black entrepreneurs have a bachelor's degree. Not in business, but in anything. These business owners were never formally taught problem-solving skills, research skills, study and learning skills, not to mention business skills. I believe that 'A lack of business acumen should never be a contributor to business failure!' And I am passionate about that!"

And I could feel it through the phone. His passion for his work was so huge, I almost had to pull the phone away from my ear.

Could I be this passionate about my business?

"Think of it!" Coach exclaimed. "An employee loses their job, and they get another job. A business owner loses his/her business, and lives are ruined. That business owner has maxed out all their credit cards, taken a second on their home, and borrowed from friends and family, only to lose it all. Families are broken apart, marriages are shattered, and lives are destroyed. We aim to reverse the statistics of small business failure by 'Creating an opportunity for all businesses to succeed!' Do you get it now?"

"Yes, I believe I do." I really was starting to get it, and I could feel excitement surfacing again. "First comes the story, and then the statement. A Vision Statement without the story is just clever words in print. It is the story that gets people excited. Okay, now I have to write my story, right?"

"Whoa, whoa, whoa, Ruben. I can appreciate your eagerness to get started, but let's stay at 30,000 feet and continue with the evaluation. You can, however, start a list of action items for follow-up on your own, should we decide you are not a candidate for my program, or for us, should we decide you qualify and you join one of my Clubs."

"Okay, I just feel like I want to act on this before I lose it." I'm sure my voice was distracted and hurried as I scribbled some quick notes, so that I had something to start with when the call was over.

"I understand. Shall we move on to Core Values?"

"Sure." I was amazed at how quickly I was following Coach's major points.

The way he presents his knowledge is so easy to comprehend.

Not at all like taking a class at the local university, which I had considered doing a few years back.

Core Values define how you treat the human element in your business.

"I have already mentioned that Core Values define how you treat the human element in your business. Some companies have written policy statements that every employee signs while others simply have them posted in every office and discuss them regularly. In either case, having them written and regularly reviewed is the key to breathing life into the values. With that in mind, please rate your company on a scale of 1-5."

There was no getting around this one.

If I rate myself high, Coach will ask to see my printed Core Values. Better to be honest.

"Coach, I would rate myself a 1 in this area, as I have no Values." As soon as the words left my mouth, I wanted to pull them back in.

I have no values? Really, Ruben? What was that about?

"What I meant to say was that we, as a company, have no Values."

Crap! I did it again. Coach is going to think I am a complete idiot.

I suddenly noticed how sweaty my palm was against the receiver.

"What I really mean is..."

"I know what you mean. Let me ask you this question: If you had your Core Values defined, how would they benefit you?"

"Wow, in so many ways. We can use them when recruiting to let potential employees know what our values are up front. We can use them in staff meetings to discuss how we are setting examples of living the values. We can use them to recognize employees who conduct themselves in alignment with the company values. And that is just off the top of my head. Coach, can I ask you a question?"

"Sure, but don't be disappointed if I reply with a question to either help clarify your question or to help you discover your own answer. With those terms, do you still want to ask me your question?"

Man! Where does he come up with this brilliant stuff! There seems to be no way to corner this guy. When I grow up, I want to be like Coach!

"Yes, I still want to ask you the question. If I had a Vision and Core Values in place and alive in my business, do you think I would have kept some of the key employees I lost last year?"

"Unfortunately, we will never positively know the answer to that question. But that is the past, and you know how I feel about wasting energy on the past. Let me ask you the same question a different way: What impact do you feel a living Vision and set of Core Values will have on your future employee retention efforts?"

Wow. Asking me my own question but purposing it in the future instead of the past... That feels much better.

"I think it is going to have a very positive impact on our employee retention, customer retention, and vendor relationships and retention. I can see how this Culture stuff can make or break a company."

"Now I can get excited about that answer. Remember, the past is to learn from, just like an old textbook — once you read it and learn from it, you put it away and rarely spend energy re-reading it. Yet, the lessons you learned from it are very impactful for the future, if applied. Are you ready for the last element in Culture?"

"Let's get it on!" The pounding in my head had stopped, and I felt ready to learn what I could and get to work.

"Okay, but before we get started with Mission, let me ask you a question. It is obvious we are not going to finish today as we only have fifteen minutes left. We can do one of two things, and I will let you decide. We can agree that this is not the right time for you to consider engaging a coach like myself, or we can schedule one more meeting to finish the evaluation. What would you like to do?"

"Let's compare calendars now and schedule our next meeting. I am free tomorrow around 5:30 p.m."

"I am home and with my family every night by 5:30 p.m. May I ask you to pick another time?"

Ouch. Home, and with family. Guess that's where I should be too.

"The next time I am open is on Friday around 2:00 p.m. How is that?"

"I work half days on Friday. That is a promise I made to my wife many years ago, and I don't break promises to her. May I suggest a time?"

Ouch again. How many promises have I broken... —◉◉◉—
just in this last year?

How many
My heart sunk. *promises have I*
broken...just in
I have to turn this around. *this last year?*

"Sure, I will make the time for this. What —◉◉◉—
works for you?"

"Well, the only time I have available in the next two weeks is next Wednesday from 10:00 a.m. to noon. Beyond that, we will have to look at next month. What would you like to do?"

This is crazy. I feel like I am chasing him to have him sell me his program, and I don't even know how much it costs, or what is involved. But I know, beyond a shadow of a doubt, that he can help me.

"Coach, if that is the only time you have available, please put my name on your calendar."

"Okay, good. May I suggest you come to my office for our next meeting? Face-to-face is always better than over the phone."

"Can you come to my office? That way, I can show you my operations, and you can meet my management team and some of my employees."

"Sorry, but I cannot meet at your place. Would you like to know why?"

"Yes." I was curious.

In sales, you always go to the prospect; they don't come to you.

"Three reasons. One, I don't ever travel to a prospective customer's office. In fact, I have never seen the four walls of 80% of my clients' businesses. Just a rule I have. Two, my calendar is booked right before you and immediately after you. I simply don't have the time for travel, and three, in order for you to be completely open and honest with me, I need to get you out of your office, where you are the king, and into my environment. Neutral ground, so to speak." He was so matter-of-fact, and yet kind. "So, here are our options. We don't meet (you won't hurt my feelings), we meet at my office, or we continue via phone. Any of those three options are completely fine with me. What would you like to do?"

If I could teach my sales people to be as courageous as Coach, our sales would go through the roof!

"Coach, I would love to come to your office. Let's book it."

"It is on my calendar in ink. How about yours? Pencil or ink?" His voice was almost playful.

I chuckled at his question.

"Ink, for sure. I will be there. Coach, can I ask you another question?"

"Sure, but you remember my rule about questions."

"I remember. Your style seems vaguely familiar. Have you ever taken a sales course from an organization called Sandler?" I just had to know where he learned his technique.

"As a matter of fact, I did. Not only did I take their program for several years, I believed in it so much that I purchased a Sandler Franchise and taught their system to hundreds of sales professionals and business owners. How interesting that you would pick up on that. I still believe that Sandler has the best sales system available, although I no longer teach it. What is your experience with Sandler?"

"I went to a boot camp but never joined their program because at the time I thought it to be too expensive. Listening to you now, I regret that decision. If my sales team and I had half of your technique, we would be unstoppable."

"Flattery will get you everywhere with me, and it is not too late to learn. Give them a second look. I am sure they can help you to improve your sales results. Let's wrap up Culture then call it a night. Fair enough?"

"Fair enough."

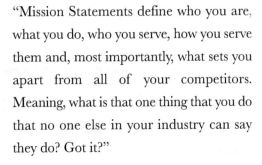

Mission Statements define who you are, what you do, who you serve, how you serve them and, most importantly, what sets you apart from all of your competitors.

"Mission Statements define who you are, what you do, who you serve, how you serve them and, most importantly, what sets you apart from all of your competitors. Meaning, what is that one thing that you do that no one else in your industry can say they do? Got it?"

"Yes, I got it. But I must be honest. I do not have a Mission Statement written down. I know it sounds ridiculous to say, but that is my reality. So, for Mission, I have to give myself another 1 rating."

That makes three 1's out of a total of three elements. What is happening here? My competitive nature is not taking this well!

I could feel the frustration in my grip on the phone.

"Okay, here is where we are. For Culture, there were a total of fifteen points, and you scored three. I know you are not pleased with that and will want to correct that between now and the next time we meet. I am not going to discourage you from acting on this emotion, but I will say that we have a four-hour session on each of those topics. To act now without the complete training may prove to be an impulsive and potentially costly error. I would suggest you keep your list of things you want to work on, and when we are done with this evaluation, you can prioritize that list and then begin to take action. You know that in the game of Chess, you gotta play strategically. We have to help you identify Your Next Move to get you the results you seek. Are you okay with that?"

Coach was spot on once again. I wanted to hit my list hard and begin getting my Culture in place.

But if we have only touched the surface of all I need to learn about each element, then it could have the same result as that accounting software I purchased. I guess it is better to wait and get all of the information before I act in haste.

"Okay, Coach, I agree with everything you said."

"Great! Then, I will see you next week Wednesday at 10:00 a.m. here at my office. Do you still have my address?"

"Yes, I still have your business card."

"Perfect. Until then, enjoy your family, and we will see you soon."

I hung up the phone and sat back in my chair. Inhaling deeply, I wondered to myself what it would be like to have Coach as my coach.

I seem to communicate well with him, he obviously knows more about business than I do, and his knowledge seems to be applicable and relevant.

With another deep inhale, I realized that my body was vibrating with energy.

And more importantly, I feel energized. I feel like I am getting that 'eye of the tiger' feeling back, and I'm excited about putting systems in place. The more I think about it, the more I want it.

As I put the notes away, I made the decision.

Somehow, Coach must see me as a viable candidate for his program. In fact, when we meet next I am going to ask him directly what he is looking for in a potential client. Yeah, that is what I am going to do.

Clicking off the lights and shutting the door, I headed home.

Wow. Home before 8:00 p.m. I'll be able to spend more than a few minutes with my family before bed tonight. I already feel better about my business, and I haven't even signed up for his program yet.

THE SECOND DISCIPLINE

GROWTH

"You are either green and growing,
or ripe and rotting…"

~ Coach ~

I arrived at Coach's office promptly at 10:00 a.m. for our appointment. The receptionist announced my presence, "Coach, Ruben Estrada is here for his meeting with you."

Even she calls him Coach?

"Please offer Ruben some coffee, and I will be down in about three minutes. I am just wrapping up my meeting." I heard Coach's request over the speakerphone.

As promised, three minutes later, Coach came walking down the spiral staircase in his lobby to greet me. At his side was a beautiful woman poised and dressed for success. She couldn't have been more than forty-five years old, although she exuded youth, vitality, and freedom. And she left no doubt as to her financial freedom with her Gucci purse, Gold Diamond Rolex, Prada shoes, and an outfit that had Rodeo Drive written all over it.

"Theodora, please meet Ruben. Ruben, Theodora." Coach made the introductions and then took one step back.

"Pleased to meet you, Ruben. Are you a friend of Coach's?" Her intentional eye contact and firm handshake reinforced my first impression.

She is a woman of power and success. Could this be one of his clients? Are they all of this caliber? If so, how am I going to fit in?

"Actually, we recently met, and he is helping me to assess my business against the Core Disciplines of Business. Today is our second meeting to complete the assessment." My mind was racing to find her file in my mental rolodex.

I know her from somewhere, but where? Theodora is such an unforgettable name.

"Oh, I remember that assessment. I almost did not qualify to be one of his clients, but I talked him into taking me anyway. Best decision he ever made because I am his star pupil and most improved client." Theodora looked up at Coach when she said this, and he gave her the same look a father would give his child to express his pride in her accomplishments.

"Hope you make it into the Club, Ruben. It will change your life," she glanced once again at Coach. "See you this weekend. Remember to bring your wife and kids. We are going to have a great time." With that, she gave Coach a hug and disappeared out the glass doors.

Coach greeted me with a hearty handshake. "Thank you for allowing me a few extra moments to finish my meeting. Let's go upstairs and get started." As we walked up the staircase, I noticed an office with an entire wall made of glass. In the center of that office was a round bar table with huge chess pieces on it.

I bet that is Coach's office.

I was right. He opened the door and stood aside, gesturing me to go in before him. "Would you like to freshen up your coffee, or would you like something else to drink? I have water, iced tea, root beer, Coke — diet or regular — or a Pellegrino?" He gestured toward the bar.

"A little more coffee would be great, thank you."

"Pick your flavor, and I will show you how to make a cup so that you can help yourself when you want more either today or in the future." Coach waited for me to choose my flavor. "My home is your home. That goes for my refrigerator as well. Feel free to help yourself," he added, pointing to a small silver and black refrigerator sitting quietly on top of a custom made cabinet. Looking around his office, it appeared that all of his furniture was custom made.

Interesting...

As Coach was showing me how to make my cup of coffee, I could not help but notice a large three-dimensional, framed structure that presented scaled down copies of numerous congressional, Senate, local government, federal, and organizational awards and plaques. There must have been a hundred different awards in this structure, each stationed in the frame at different depths.

There must have been a hundred different awards in this structure, each stationed in the frame at different depths.

This man is accomplished.

This man is accomplished.

"This is pretty impressive." I said to Coach while looking at the awards, thinking how wonderful it must be to have one's work and character acknowledged to this degree.

How does he not have an ego the size of Texas?

"Thanks. If I had it my way I would take it down, but that would break the hearts of the people who put it up. I took all my awards and put them into a box in the closet, but one day when I was out of town, my team decided to have this made and mounted. At first I was embarrassed to have it up because I believed it to be boisterous. I have come to enjoy watching new visitors take their time to scan the structure. It's a great conversation piece."

I nodded, but my mind was on other things. "Coach, before we get started, I have a few questions for you. Do you mind?" I had to ask him about his criteria about client selection, and I had to ask him about Theodora. Both topics were chewing at my mind and I would be worthless unless I had those two questions answered.

"Fire away," he gestured toward a large leather chair in front of his black marble desk. I sank into the cozy chair and hesitated for just a moment as I took in the beautiful desk.

I made a mental note to ask him about the desk's special character before I left.

"Thank you. The first question has to do with Theodora. She is so familiar to me, and I am confident I know her from somewhere."

He smiled. "Well, I cannot tell you much, because of client confidentiality, other than she owns a development company and is often on the news as a commercial development expert."

There's that fatherly pride again. I hope he feels like that about me someday.

"That's it! That is Theodora Johnson, the CEO of the Johnson Group. They are a large company. I have been trying to meet her for years, and the day she shakes my hand, I can't remember her." My voice trailed off as I realized how Coach might have taken my statement and then felt the weight of her words hit me.

Wow, if she almost did not qualify as a client, where do I stand?

"Thank you for that. My second question has to do with your qualifications for a client. I really feel like you can help me, but I am not sure what you are looking for from me." I recognized, once I paused, that I did not ask a question.

Why do I ask questions in the form of statements when I am uncomfortable?

"Although you did not ask me a direct question, can I assume you want to know my criteria for client selection?"

He never assumes. He always confirms.

I was struck again by the way he engaged me. His rules of interaction were so clear, and he was always confirming, reassuring, paraphrasing, and getting permission.

It's amazing how safe it makes me feel, even when I'm at the edge of my comfort zone.

"That would put my mind at great ease." I felt relieved, as I didn't want to have to keep wondering whether I would make the cut or not.

"That is a fair request. Let me make a proposal. I will tell you my criteria for client selection, and then we can finish the assessment with a clear understanding that we will both decide if you are a candidate. Fair enough?"

"Very fair."

"My criteria are simple. First of all, I must have an open spot for a new client. Secondly, I must feel that the business owner is fully committed to change. Thirdly, the business owner must agree to the following: 1) to attend a four-hour training session and a private one-on-one coaching session with me, or one of my coaches, every month for two years; 2) to be held accountable and monitored via our proprietary online "Coaching Journal" which monitors the high impact initiatives the client is working on and also monitors the businesses Key Performance Indicators; and 3) to pay the required Club membership. Membership ranges between $12,000 to $32,000 for two years, depending on the Club. Has anything I have said scared you yet?"

$32,000 for two years? Are you kidding me? I blew $100,000 on a consulting firm in one shot.

"No, nothing scares me yet. Are the Club meetings on the weekend or evenings?" I hoped they were because my weekdays were booked solid.

"Why do you ask that question?" He smiled like he already knew.

Uh-oh.

"Well, it's kind of hard for me to get away during the work week."

"Hmmm, that could be a deal breaker. All of our Club meetings are held during the work week, during working hours."

Did I just offer my advice to Coach in order to get my needs met?

"Why is that, Coach? I have to believe that there are many business owners like myself who cannot get away from their business during the week. You may be missing a large market there."

I felt a bit manipulative and worried about how he would respond.

Did I just offer my advice to Coach in order to get my needs met?

I felt a bit manipulative and worried about how he would respond.

"If you recall an earlier conversation, I mentioned that we don't work past 5:00 p.m. on weekdays, and not at all on weekends, or after noon on Friday. The source of that work schedule is one of our Core Values that state: "We believe in Faith, Family, Friends, then Fortune." We never compromise our Core Values. Also, a key behavior of a successful CEO is that he or she makes time to work ON the business." He emphasized the word ON. "In fact, this is one of the most important behaviors of any successful CEO. For those business owners who simply cannot attend a work week, work day session, I am sure there are other programs to help them. They would not qualify as a client. Is this a deal breaker? It's okay if it is; we will still complete the assessment," he explained without apology.

"No. If that is what it takes, then I will have to make it happen."

Why am I selling Coach on taking me on as a client? This is the opposite of how I was trained to do sales. It is almost as though Coach does not need my business but is willing to consider me if I meet his criteria.

"Just to make sure we are on the same page, can you tell me what we have just agreed to?" Coach asked.

"Sure, I have committed to meet all your client conditions, and after the assessment, we will both decide if I am a candidate for one of your Clubs."

"Great, thank you for bringing up the qualifications to become a client. It will make it much easier for us to make a decision after the assessment. Speaking of that, we should get started. I have us scheduled to meet for two hours. Are you still good with that?"

"Yes, I have scheduled the entire afternoon to meet with you if necessary," I offered.

"Thank you. However, I have a lunch commitment, and then I am delivering a keynote address for the 'State of the County' this evening. Are you going?"

"I saw the invitation but did not make a reservation. Can I just go and pay at the door?" I did not want to miss the opportunity to hear him speak. In fact, I kind of wanted to just follow Coach around for a month and soak up all of his knowledge and wisdom. "What are you going to talk about?"

"First, I believe you can pay at the door, or you can come as my guest," he offered. "My talk is on social consciousness of the business executive and a model I call 'My Three Causes,' that is comprised of three defined causes aimed at strengthening our regional economic ecosystem. All three causes are choices of the business owner/executive and, when implemented concurrently, are entrepreneurial accelerators. But that is a conversation for another day. I think we should get started. What do you think?"

"I think I would love to hear more about 'My Three Causes,' but I can get that tonight. You are right, we should get started with the next Discipline," I said.

So he is not just a business coach, but a civic and community leader. It seems that everything he does touches the business community directly. Talk about clarity of purpose and focus. I need to make a note to ask Coach about that when I am his client.

"Alright, what is the next Discipline?" Coach asked.

"Well, if I am reading this chart correctly, the next Discipline would be Growth."

"That is correct. You see, there are six operational Disciplines, each represented by one of the pieces in the game of chess."

I think I finally caught Coach.

"Coach, I know there are only six pieces to a chess game, and I see all six of them on the chart, but you have seven Disciplines. I understand the metaphor of business being strategy and how each Discipline, like each chess piece, has its unique capabilities and purpose, but what is the chess piece for Culture?"

—◆◆◆—

There are six operational Disciplines, each represented by one of the pieces in the game of chess.

—◆◆◆—

"Great observation. Very few people notice that when we first meet."

I knew I caught him.

"Let me ask you a question," he said. "Can you play the game of chess without the chess board? Even if you have all the pieces?"

"Well, no. Without the board, you have no foundation for the game. You need the board to line up all the pieces and to monitor that they are being used properly." The moment I said that, it clicked.

Oh…I see…

"Tell me what you are thinking." He appeared pleased with what must have been a look of sudden clarity on my face.

"I just got it. Culture is the chess board. Culture sets the foundation for the entire company, sets the rules of conduct, and monitors that each Discipline is doing what it is supposed to do."

"Very insightful. You are picking this up very fast. Now, did you bring our Core Disciplines of Business chart with you?"

I have so much to learn. Breathe, Ruben. You have someone to help you figure this out.

"I did." And the moment I pulled it out, I began to feel overwhelmed by what I didn't know.

I have so much to learn. Breathe, Ruben. You have someone to help you figure this out.

"Alright, let's discuss why Growth is a Discipline of business. Do you have some ideas?"

"Well, there is that saying that 'nothing happens in business until the sale is made.' I believe that to be true. If my company stopped focusing on Sales, we would eventually go out of business. I think this is the most important Discipline of business."

"Outstanding. So you understand why this is the first operational Discipline, second only to Culture?"

"Yes, I believe I do. Sales has always been very important to our company, and I think we manage this Discipline very well. In fact, I would take a guess that my total points for this Discipline are going to be much higher than Culture." I was the master salesperson for my company, and if anyone knew Sales and how to make sales, I did.

I am going to do well with this Discipline.

I could feel my confidence re-emerging and sat up a little straighter.

"I love your confidence and eagerness. Let's briefly talk through each element, and you can rate yourself on how well you have developed systems for each. Do you remember the rating we used?"

"Yes, scale of 1-5, with 5 being strong systems…written systems."

"Perfect. Let's talk first about the element of Sales. So, do you have a Sales system?"

"Well, yes?"

I do, don't I? Why do I feel so incompetent here? It's like I haven't been in business at all for the last few years.

"Great. Here is a blank piece of paper. Please draw it out for me."

What? Draw it out? No one has ever asked me to do that.

"Well, actually, since I close the majority of the deals, I have it in my head."

"So take a moment and draw out what you have in your head. If you can't do that, then I must ask you what happens to your Sales if you get injured for an extended period of time and are pulled out of the business."

He got me again. Here I am thinking that I got this one nailed just because I have always done well with Sales, but he is right. Without a system, I will never be able to replicate myself in this element.

"Okay, Coach, can you give me an example of a Sales system?"

"Yes, but before I do, let me say that most companies do not have this element well-defined. So, again, you are not alone."

I love how he has a way of making me feel okay even when I know I blew it. If I could learn to do that with my people, how much more productive would they be?

I thought back to a meeting I had a few days earlier with my Production manager. He had miscalculated materials for an important job and, as a result, cost us $10,000.00. When he left our meeting, his head was down, and I could tell he was hurt by some of the things I had said.

"Have you heard the business rule that 'all work is a process'?" Coach asked.

"Yes, and I do believe that to be true as well."

"So, if that is true, then Sales must have a process that is applicable to any business. I am not talking technique. I am talking CEO level systems management. Here is an example of what I mean."

Coach drew six circles on a blank sheet of paper then proceeded to connect them with arrows with the last circle connecting with the first.

"Okay, in the first circle, let's call this a suspect. But we must have a concrete definition of what a suspect is for your business. So, tell me, who are your suspects?"

"Honestly, anybody can buy my products."

"Okay, I am financially ruined, just filed for bankruptcy, I lost my home and all of my assets, and my wife left me. I committed a felony and will be going to prison for thirty-five years next week. I have been diagnosed with a terminal disease and have been given six months to live. Am I a suspect for your products?"

"Well. No!"

"Thank God you have *some* criteria. Let's start there and work our way back towards discovering who your real suspects are. Listen, you can spend thousands of dollars marketing to unqualified suspects. Why? Do you know that Rolls Royce,

Lamborghini and other high-end auto manufacturers have a direct mail program? Do you know that many of us never receive their direct mail? Do you know why?"

"Well, I would guess that we are not their suspects."

"Exactly! Every business has a target suspect, market, or demographic they market to. The more specific you are with your suspect criteria, the more effective your Marketing campaigns are. For example, our target market, or suspects, are privately-owned businesses where the owner is active in the business. The business revenues are between half a million and $50 million, and generally the business is within twenty-six miles from the coach's office, unless it is an online client. Now that is pretty specific. That does not mean that we refuse service to people or organizations outside of that definition; it is a guideline for data and campaign management. Get it?"

"I got it. What about the other circles?"

After this meeting, I am going to run back to my office and have my Accounting department complete a profile of our top 100 active clients as a guideline to begin defining our suspect criteria. With that information, we can get very focused with our Marketing efforts. Wow, all of these years, all of the money and time we invested in marketing to everyone versus a targeted suspect. No wonder we have not had results! This one alone is worth the price of his Club membership.

"Okay. Let's go through them pretty quickly."

In the next circles, Coach wrote the words "Prospect," then

"Opportunity," then "Sales," then "Customer," then "Referral," which fed the suspect circle, and the process started all over again. Coach emphasized the importance of having clear definitions for each circle and then a list of activities between the circles that moved the process forward.

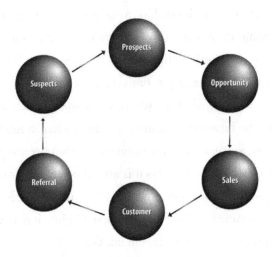

Wow. If I had a well-defined Sales system, my team and I would all be clear on what we were working on, and what leads we're moving through the funnel. This one is HUGE for me. Maybe I need to take this more slowly.

"Coach, you mentioned a four-hour club meeting. Will we spend four hours learning the entire Discipline, or is it one session per element?"

"Great question. Each Club meeting provides training on a single element. With twenty-seven elements, you understand now why the program is two years, minimum."

"I can stop here and make the commitment to join your club today. Just with the discussion about Culture and now Growth, I have enough to keep me busy for months."

"That is encouraging, but remember, we have not talked at all about *how* to implement these elements in your business. Nor have we thoroughly trained you on the few elements we have discussed." He studied me momentarily. "Remember, the spirit of this assessment is to get a complete overview of where your business may need improvement via systems. Neither of us could possibly know your next move at this point."

"Okay, I am just ready to start implementing." I understood that I needed to do this strategically.

But would it really hurt for me to do some market research?

"I understand. Now, with your newfound knowledge about building a Sales system, how would you rate the element of Sales for your company?"

"Funny, before we started talking, I was confident we would be a 5, but now, understanding what a Sales system looks like, I have to say we are a 1."

"Are you sure about that?"

"Sad to say, yes." I felt terrible that my strongest area got such a low rating.

I now know, beyond a shadow of a doubt, that I need to join the Club.

"What is the second element on the chart under Growth?"

"Marketing," I answered.

"Okay, tell me what you know about systems for Marketing."

"Well, to be totally honest, I don't really know. We do spend a lot of money on Marketing, but I don't believe we have any systems in place." I felt my stomach starting to churn with anger again.

"All right, let me help you out a bit. Every effective Marketing program has systems built around the three fundamental goals of Marketing. Do you know what those goals are?"

"No." I felt so much conflict inside of me.

I am definitely on the edge of my comfort zone. Excited. Overwhelmed. This is so much to learn...so quickly!

"Here they are. The goals of Marketing are:

- #1: To increase **visibility** within the market place that you serve.

- #2: To develop **credibility** within the market place that you serve.

- #3: To demonstrate **ability** within the market place that you serve.

"For example, we have a very large database of suspects who get a weekly email called the CEO Rule of the week. This e-blast goes out every Tuesday without fail. (Visibility.) In the email we offer a valuable Rule for the CEO (Credibility) and within the email are video testimonials from clients who are succeeding in our programs along with invitations to webinars and workshops we are hosting for business owners (demonstration of Ability). With this example, how would you rate the element of Marketing for your business?"

"1."

Again!

My blood was officially boiling.

"Ruben, don't worry about the ratings. You are learning things for the first time. For four years, you have worked hard to build a successful business, and done millions in revenue. You did all of that without this knowledge of systems. Imagine what your business can look like in a few years with all of these systems in place."

For four years, you have worked hard to build a successful business, and done millions in revenue. You did all of that without this knowledge of systems. Imagine what your business can look like in a few years with all of these systems in place."

Coach was right. I was being too hard on myself.

We do have a good company that is poised to grab market share. All we need to do is educate ourselves on these Core Disciplines of Business and implement the systems.

I was beginning to get encouraged again. Coach's words echoed in my mind: "Focus on the future, Ruben, not the past."

I am getting a pretty clear picture of what needs to be done to significantly impact my organization.

"Okay, Coach. Let's continue with this assessment."

"The next element is Advertising. The system here is pretty straightforward," he sat back and clasped his hands behind his head, conveying complete ease. "For every Advertising dollar spent, what is the ROI? This system is more about measurement of frequency and defined desired results. How would you rate this element?"

"Well, we don't really do much advertising, but the little we do pay for, we are not tracking. So I would rate us about a 2 here."

"Great, but can you tell me what systems you have written for your Advertising efforts?"

"Oh yeah, well, we don't have anything written down."

Ouch! Another 1? If this were a tax audit, I would be going to prison!

"Are you ready to talk about the last element in Growth?"

"Yes, but I must tell you up front, I know very little about Branding systems." I was trying to buffer the inevitable 1 rating that was coming.

"Well, can you tell me what you do know about Branding and why it is important to a business?" Coach was going to pull something out of me one way or another.

"What I know about Branding is that a company should have a logo, and that's about it."

"Not bad. Can you tell me why a company needs a logo?"

"Well, I assume it is to help people recognize who you are."

"Right again. Companies will typically brand three things — their logo, their slogan, and their message. The logo is important because people think in pictures, not in words. Our logo is the six chess pieces. The reason it is important to brand your slogan is because people also think in emotions. Think about it, when I am speaking at a conference and the topic is Branding, I will ask the audience to think of a word when they hear the word TREE. The responses I get are branch, leaf, trunk, paper, etc. (all images) or environment, clean air, recycle, etc. (all emotions). The logo is the picture, the slogan is the emotion. What is the logo, the picture, for Nike? The Swoosh. What is the slogan, or the emotion? 'Just do it!'" He peered at me intently, making sure I was with him on this.

"Branding your message is important because the message explains the brand and what it stands for. Once all three are standardized, then every printed document, business card, marketing collateral, website and so on, must promote the same picture, emotion, and message. Recently, I was working with a client who brought me a sample of his business card, marketing brochure, and other materials, and was amazed at how inconsistent his brand had become. Listen, your business is your Brand. So Branding systems are all about consistency of brand promotion and standardization of brand use. So, on a scale of 1 - 5, where are you with your brand?"

Finally, one that we can say we are doing well with.

"We are about a 3.5 here. We have standardized all of our print collateral and business cards to promote one logo and slogan. The thing we need to standardize is our messaging. Can you give me an example of that?"

"Our standard message is: 'We help the small to mid-sized business owner to think, act, and perform like a successful CEO. We accomplish this through training, coaching, and monitoring around our Core Disciplines of Business.'"

"I will need to spend a bit more time with that one." I was inwardly groaning, and I'm sure it was obvious on my face. A poker face, I am not.

"Yes, but it seems like you got your logo and slogan nailed. Great job." He glanced at the chart, and pointed to it. "Okay, that wraps up Growth. Can you add up your ratings and compare them to the ideal of 20?"

"Sure, I have 3+3.5, so we are at 6.5 for Growth."

"Excellent. Now imagine your company at a 20. Where could you be?"

"We would be a completely different company! How exciting!" I really could see it. I could see me documenting our Sales process and training others to produce at my levels.

That would bring me great freedom.

"Nice, before we move on to Client Retention, can we freshen up your coffee or get you another beverage?"

"Can I get a cold drink? The coffee was wonderful, but you got me all heated up."

"Help yourself, Ruben. You are at home."

I slowly got up and walked to the refrigerator. Opening it, I was surprised to see the variety of vanity waters, old-school Root Beer bottles, Pellegrino, Diet Coke, and a variety of all-natural juices.

This guy is top-shelf all the way.

I grabbed an all-natural juice and quickly sat back down, excited to talk about Client Retention.

I am really enjoying this.

THE THIRD DISCIPLINE

CLIENT RETENTION

"Client Retention IS growth..."

~ Coach ~

As I sat looking out the window, waiting for Coach to return from a short break, I tried to prepare myself for the next conversation.

Client Retention. How are we doing with Client Retention? I wonder if he needs to know that the day I met him, I was on my way to try to save a client.

I started to feel the frustration, and even shame, rise up again.

Ruben, you are on the edge of your comfort zone. You don't know what you don't know. And, if you hadn't been in that mess, you wouldn't have met Coach. There are no coincidences. Focus on the future.

Coach returned and interrupted my pep talk. "Here is an important CEO Rule for you to remember, Ruben, 'Retention is growth.' Can you tell me what you think that means?"

"Sure, if you are losing clients out the back door faster than you can bring them in the front, then you will have negative growth." I knew about this one firsthand.

We have been losing clients and are being told that it is because of our prices.

I didn't understand that because our margins are very tight, and for a competitor to consistently under-price us, it would mean they are giving it away for free.

There has to be something else going on.

"Excellent. You are exactly right. It is amazing how much measurement of Sales companies do, yet when I ask those same companies to produce similar reports for Client Retention, they look at me like I have two heads. Why do you think that is, Ruben?"

Reports?!? I was looking at Coach like he had two heads.

Reports?!? I was looking at Coach like he had two heads.

"Well, your story matches us exactly. We have tons of reports for Sales activities and Sales made, but I cannot tell you of one report we have to measure Client Retention," I answered sheepishly.

Retention is growth. That is so true. So why hadn't I thought of this before?

"I appreciate your honesty once again. Now let's assess your business against the four elements in Client Retention." He pointed to the chart. "Those elements are Customer Service, Customer Appreciation, Customer Feedback, and Accounts Receivable. Now I get many business owners who would argue that AR's should be under Finance, but I push back every time. Think of it this way. The only two reasons that a customer does not pay are: one, they don't value the relationship, in which case Customer Service needs to get out and strengthen that relationship; or two, they don't have any money, in which case they should not be a customer. I continue to argue that AR's is a function of Client Retention, not Finance. Let's start with Customer Service. What systems do you have for Customer Service?"

"Well, if a customer calls in, that call gets documented, distributed to the person who is responsible for that account, and tracked for resolution. We can see what client issues are outstanding and what has been resolved. In every instance, once the issue is resolved, our Customer Service team calls the customer to verify that we really took care of their issue. Now, although we have pretty good practices here, those practices are not written down in the form of a system," I answered confidently.

Finally, one that we do well.

"Ruben, that is exactly what I would have coached you to put in place if you did not have a proven system. Once you get it written up, you can give that one a very high rating. What would you rate it today?"

"I would give us a 4.5." I didn't try to hide the pride in my voice.

"I agree. Let's move onto Client Appreciation. Tell me, Ruben, what systems do you have in place for this element?"

————

————

"Honestly, Coach, before I met you, I had never heard the term Client Appreciation before. I cannot say I have any experience with this element." My voice faltered again.

"Fair enough. Let me take a moment to explain this element for you by asking you a few questions. Can you tell me what you have budgeted for marketing this year?"

"Yes. I believe we have budgeted $23,000."

Believe? I squirmed. *I should know for sure what my budget is.*

"Impressive. Now can you tell me what you have budgeted for Sales salaries and commissions?"

"Yes, we have ten reps at $65,000 each. So let's say $700,000 with taxes and benefits."

Wow. $700K on a team that is not closing any deals? All they do is generate the lead for me to close. Man, something is very wrong with my Sales system. Note to self: FIX THIS!

"You seem to know exactly how much you have budgeted to get new clients. Now, can you tell me what you have budgeted to *keep* the clients you have?"

What do you mean by a budget to keep clients? Who does that?

He had two heads again.

"Well, no, but we do take clients to lunch once in a while."

Actually, I take clients to lunch once in a great while.

"That's good, but not really a system. A solid Client Appreciation system has a schedule of events or programs designed to demonstrate to your clients how much you appreciate the relationship."

We give outstanding service to demonstrate how much we appreciate our clients. Isn't that enough?

As Coach continued, it became very clear that it wasn't enough.

"For example, we host bi-monthly Client Appreciation events. Some are extravagant where others are less extravagant. We host an annual Cinco de Mayo event and have over 750 people attend. It is a complete family event with funnel cakes, face painting, piñatas, water toys, bounce houses, and a photo booth for the kids. Next month we are having our annual skeet-shooting outing where we select twenty clients to join us at the shooting range to shoot clay ducks. You see, providing excellent service is no longer a sales pitch; it is an expectation."

Ouch! He read my mind again.

As if to give me the final one-two punch, he added, "And in today's increasingly competitive business climate, we need to go above and beyond to strengthen our relationships with our clients. So, our system is an annual calendar with every event predetermined and a list of clients we intend to invite to each event. Call it 'marketing to existing clients.' Throughout the year, we follow that schedule. Got it?"

"Got it," I nodded and made a note in my journal. "I need to develop a calendar of events or programs that would allow us to further strengthen our relationships. For those clients who are out of state, we can host a private social at the annual industry conference or do other things throughout the year. We need to budget each event, track who attends each event, and keep account records for this expense to track how much we are spending on Client Appreciation."

Why haven't I thought of hosting an event and inviting our clients to attend? That is a brilliant idea! I want to start this next month. But then again, everything I have learned so far, I want to start next month.

"You really are a fast learner!" he chuckled. "How would you rate your company on this element?"

"Given that we are not doing anything at the moment, I would have to give us a 1." For some reason, rating my company a 1 was not so bad any longer. My focus was beginning to shift from what we were not doing to the possibilities that came with implementing these new systems.

Already, I can see tremendous potential, and we were only half way through the second Discipline. Where was Coach four years ago when we were just getting started?

"Can you tell me how this element, when fully implemented, would benefit your organization?" His eyes sparked with genuine curiosity.

"I can see a big party with fifty of our current clients and prospective clients interacting and having fun. I can see us getting to know our clients at a deeper level and truly building relationships with them. Yes, I see this as becoming a significant part of our Client Retention strategy."

There have been numerous unfulfilled suggestions to get together with my clients. Almost every time I am on the phone, we end the call saying, 'We should get together for coffee or lunch,' but rarely follow through. This would be a great way to catch up with many clients at once.

"Should you become a client, I will look forward to seeing you and your family at some of our Client Appreciation events. Speaking of that, do you mind if I ask the names of your family?"

"Sure, my wife's name is Kathy and we have two children. Our daughter is Judy, and our son is Ronnie." I could not remember the last time I was asked about my family during a business meeting.

This is kind of refreshing.

"What a coincidence — my wife is also named Kathy. How did you meet your wife?"

There was a day, not too long ago, when I used to laugh a lot. What happened to those days? I WILL get them back!

"We met in El Paso, Texas. She was a corporate buyer, and I was a sales rep."

"Ah, a match made in heaven."

"Yeah, it was a 'one-call close,' so to speak." I smiled, remembering the first time we met.

Coach laughed at my last comment, and I noted how healthy and sincere his laugh was. I could tell that he likes to laugh a lot.

There was a day, not too long ago, when I used to laugh a lot. What happened to those days? I WILL get them back!

Coach looked back at the Core Disciplines of Business, indicating that we needed to get back on track. "Ready for the next element?"

"Yes, I am." I sat up straight in my chair with my note pad in hand, waiting for the next lesson.

"The next element in Client Retention is Customer Feedback systems. Can you tell me what you think that means, and if you currently have any such systems in place?" I could tell by the look on his face that we were definitely back to business.

"I can tell you what I think it means, but we don't currently have any systems in place for getting feedback from our clients. From time to time, we do get an unsolicited testimonial from a client, but that is about it." My interest was at full attention on this one.

"Fair enough. So tell me, how you would explain the element of Customer Feedback systems?" Coach peered at me intently.

"I would say that these systems were designed to get comprehensive surveys from each active client to learn, from their point of view, what they like about our service, what they don't like about our service, and possibly some ideas for new things we could be offering them. How is that?"

Man, some of this stuff is so obvious. All these years in business, and I never thought to put together a survey? Maybe I would not have lost so many clients if I had been getting their feedback on a regular basis. This is not rocket science!

"Very well said! Now I want to write down your definition of Customer Feedback."

Wow! I have Coach writing my ideas down now!

"Just to synchronize our use of words, let me offer two distinct methods of getting valuable information from your clients. One would be a survey and the other would be a Customer Feedback interview. The differences are distinct, as a survey is typically multiple questions designed primarily for Marketing purposes, whereas a Customer Feedback interview usually has no more than five questions specifically designed to determine a company

CSI. Do you know what CSI stands for?"

"Crime Scene Investigation?" I offered. Coach laughed again at my comment.

"Good try. I guess that was not a fair question to ask. CSI stands for a company's Customer Satisfaction Index. However, if your company is bleeding because of excessive client losses, then Crime Scene Investigation would be a better definition."

Do you know what CSI stands for?

"Crime Scene Investigation?" I offered. Coach laughed again at my comment.

We both laughed at that.

Man, it feels good to laugh when talking about business. It just feels good to laugh again. When was the last time I laughed at work, with my wife, or in play with my kids?

"Allow me to offer a bit more explanation, and then we can move on." He propped his elbows on the desk and leaned forward. "In every business, there are typically 3-5 unique service offerings that set that business apart from their competitors. The goal of the Customer Feedback system is to validate that those unique offerings are well-received and valued by your clients, and that the business is fulfilling its promise when delivering those offerings."

For some reason, I couldn't process what he had just said. And I noticed that I was looking at Coach with my head tilted slightly to one side, the same way my dog looks at me when he does not quite understand me.

Coach picked up on my confusion. "All right, I can see that you don't quite follow what I am saying, so let me give you an example of what our Customer Feedback system looks like. We train, coach, and monitor our clients with the aim to assist them to fully learn and implement the Core Disciplines of Business in their organizations. This is what sets us apart from other companies. So, our Customer Feedback Interviews focus only around those three unique service offerings. We ask each client to assess each of the three on a scale of 1 - 5 with a 5 being completely satisfied. If they score us less than a 5, we ask them what we could do to become a 5. You following me?"

This was beginning to make so much sense, but I was not sure how I would implement it in my business. "Yes, but I don't know what my unique service offerings are?"

"We are not here to answer that question today. That would take much more time than we have. At this moment, my goal is to introduce you to the element, only. Are you okay?"

"Yes, but why do you have to keep telling me that? Once I get something that can benefit my business, I want to quickly move towards implementation. Is that wrong?"

"Not wrong, but dangerous. Tell me, what is the danger of implementing something you don't fully understand?"

I paused for a moment. "Well, it takes time, people, and money to implement new systems, and if it is implemented wrong, then you may have wasted that money. Also, the people who took the time to implement the system could get discouraged and not want to re-implement it at a later date."

———*∿∿*———

"Anything else?" He raised an eyebrow, obviously sensing that I had more to say.

I am beginning to see your strategy. You want me to fully understand my business before taking action on any of these 'lessons learned.'

———*∿∿*———

"I guess if I went back and tried to implement too many new systems at once, I could frustrate my team. There is a strategy for managing change." As I answered Coach's question, I began to relax about not having to rush back and implement all that I was learning. It was kind of like giving me permission to hold off and take my time to implement this change. I saw why Coach insisted we complete the assessment of all twenty-seven elements. He wanted me to see the entire "big picture," so to speak.

I nodded. "I am beginning to see *your* strategy. You want me to fully understand my business before taking action on any of these 'lessons learned.' Is that correct?"

"You got it. Let's wrap up Customer Feedback then we can move on to the last element in Client Retention. Okay?"

"Let's go."

"All right. Let's say you ask your customers for feedback and you see that you have lots of 4's and only a few 3's in one key area. And with each client who rated you less than a 4, you asked them what you could do to be a 5. What do you do to improve that CSI?"

"Well, if what the customer suggested is realistic, we would have to take that seriously into consideration."

Ouch again! How many emergency meetings have we held recently to try and figure out how to stop the client losses when all we have to do is get out there and ask them?

"Correct! Far too often businesses try to figure out what their customers want through trial and error when your customers will tell you if you ask. Rating?"

"This one really has to be a -5, Coach."

"Let's give it a 1 and move on, okay?"

"I'm good with that."

Man! What a simple process. If we did this regularly with each of our customers, we could post our CSI up on the wall, break our service department into teams, and create some internal recognition for improved CSI.

The more I thought of this, the more I got excited. I took another sip of the wonderfully tasting natural drink.

"I get it. You don't have to figure out how to improve that CSI; the customers have already told you. That's amazing, yet so simple!"

"You will find that much of what we talk about is not complicated or new. Often it is just making the business owner aware of the element, providing some in-depth training, and then strategically coaching and monitoring the implementation. That is when the magic happens."

I was beginning to see why the Clubs were two-year programs. There is so much to learn and implement, one simply could not do it all in a few short weeks or months.

"With this review of every element, I am getting more and more excited about the future of my company and, more importantly, I am beginning to understand what 'Begin with the End in Mind' means for me. As for this element, I must give us a 1 simply because we have no Customer Feedback systems in place."

"Excellent! Now let's wrap up the last element in Client Retention, which is Accounts Receivable. Can you tell me about your AR systems?"

> *"You will find that much of what we talk about is not complicated or new. Often it is just making the business owner aware of the element, providing some in-depth training, and then strategically coaching and monitoring the implementation. That is when the magic happens."*

"All of our customers pay off of invoices with an agreed upon net 30. Although we have it in our agreements to charge interest for invoices beyond 30 days, we never do. In fact, our biggest cash problem is outstanding ARs. I have two full-time employees whose entire job is to collect 60 — 90 day plus receivables. I am not really sure how you can systematize this, Coach. If we cut our customer off due to non-payment, my fear is that we will lose the customer." What I left out was how a lack of system in this area was crippling my business.

If we were able to collect all of our monies on time, we would be in a completely different position with our bank. Every month, we are maxing out our line of credit due to a lack of Cash Flow.

"Many business owners feel the exact same way about their AR's. They fear that customers would get upset if you enforced your payment terms or, worse yet, that they would quit service. But let me ask you this: If you had solid and consistent Customer Service, Client Appreciation, and Customer Feedback systems in place, do you feel you would have the same AR challenges?"

"When you put it that way, no."

"Why not?"

"Because if we were consistently providing excellent customer service by responding to our clients calls quickly and resolving their issues promptly, if we went deeper in our relationships by deploying good Client Appreciation systems, and if we conducted regular Customer Feedback Interviews, I think our relationship with our clients would be at a completely different level. They would have a much deeper appreciation for our relationship and thus be more willing to pay us first when they have to make delayed vendor payment decisions. In short, they would become our friends, and friends take care of friends first."

Turning clients into friends? That sounds amazing....

"I agree completely. Because of our Client Retention systems, our clients call us when they need some extra time to pay a bill versus us having to call them regarding outstanding AR's. I know it seems a bit unrealistic, but it can happen with your business. Now, as for AR systems, they shift from simply collection policies to a more complete process that begins with how payment terms are negotiated at the point of sale. Yes, I said negotiated. In today's rapidly shifting world of technology, credit card and bank transfer methods are becoming more acceptable. Also, an open and honest conversation about payment terms and consequences up front, followed by a complete Client Retention plan, make it easier to enforce collection efforts when and if necessary. Remember, if you are using all of the Client Retention systems, a customer who is unwilling or unable to pay your bill is not a customer — they are a liability. How do you feel about that last CEO Rule?"

"It makes all the sense in the world. If I am doing all the things we talked about and a customer is not paying their bill, then I cannot be afraid of implementing our collection policies and charging interest and/or disrupting service. And if they quit after all that, then they were not going to be a customer for long anyway. In fact, if they quit with just 30 days past due, it is much better than quitting with 160 days of uncollected AR's that we wind up writing off at the end of the year. Yes, that makes sense to me."

Could it really be possible for my company to get to a point where all of our customers were paying their bills on time? I was starting to believe that it was possible.

Could it really be possible for my company to get to a point where all of our customers were paying their bills on time? I was starting to believe that it was possible.

"How would you rate your company on a scale of 1 - 5 here?"

"I would proudly give us a 1. I say 'proudly' because I can clearly see how we can greatly improve this element." I was beginning to see how having a greater awareness of where my systems were lacking was more important than getting a good score.

"Nice, now, what was your overall rating for this Discipline?" Coach asked.

"I total up to a 7.5 out of a potential 15."

"Very good. Now, let's get a cold drink and start with the next element."

We walked away from his black marble top desk to get a cold drink. I decided it was a good moment to ask about the characteristic of the desk that had caught my eye that morning. It did not look like a desk at all. In fact, it looked like it belonged in someone's kitchen.

"Would you mind telling me about your desk? I mean, it looks like an old fashioned kitchen table."

"I had it made in memory of the table we had when I was a kid. I used to do my best thinking at that kitchen table. Like when I was doing my homework or just sitting there with my chin on my hands, daydreaming about my friends, or my future. Have you noticed that the table is about five inches higher than a normal table?"

Now that he mentioned it, I remembered a moment where I felt like a little kid sitting at that desk.

I thought it was just my frustration with feeling small in my business.

Coach continued, without waiting for my answer. "That is because I wanted to be able to cross my arms on the table, rest my chin in my hands, and daydream when at my desk, just like I did when I was a kid. Now, don't you go telling everyone my secret about that desk." He smiled and finished pouring his cold drink.

It seems that everything Coach does is deliberate. From his custom desk that was a replica of his childhood dinner table and the custom chessboard, to the Core Disciplines of Business. Everything has a purpose and a story. I want to learn more about Coach.

THE FOURTH DISCIPLINE

ADMINISTRATION

*"Administration is the glue that holds
the company together..."*

~ Coach ~

"By now, you probably have the process down," he said, sitting back in his chair. "Tell me what you think of when you think Administration." Coach didn't miss a beat, moving me into the next element.

"Actually, I have never given much thought to this. In the past, Administration was just one of those necessary 'things' we had to do in business. To me, Administration was a receptionist, office manager, some filing, and that was about it. Looking at the Core Disciplines of Business, it seems to be much more. I see the elements of Human Resources, Communications, Calendar and Scheduling, and General Office. I can hardly wait to see what I will learn here."

Honestly, I thought it was here that Coach would lose me.

I mean, how exciting can Administration be?

"Ruben, where Sales and Client Retention fund the business, Administration is the glue that holds everything together. Let's dive right into it and get started with Human Resources. You know the routine. Go ahead. The floor is yours."

How exciting can Administration be?

"Well, we are not large enough to have a full Human Resources department. We do have quite a bit of hiring, and try to do performance evaluations once per year, but that is about it. As for HR systems, I really can't think of any." I hated to admit this.

"That's very common." Coach slid a blank piece of paper in front of me.

What is he up to now?

"All right. Now," Coach continued, "in the center of the paper, draw a circle and label it Job Descriptions."

I did that, but got the feeling I was not going to like where this was going.

"Now, you have job descriptions for all of the positions in your company, don't you?"

I knew I wasn't going to like where this was going…

"Everyone in our company knows their job pretty well. I have never really seen the need for job descriptions. They seem to be so limiting. I want my people to do what is necessary, even if it is outside of their primary job." I could hardly take *myself* seriously.

How does he not laugh out loud at some of this crap?

Coach did not respond to this. He just sat back in his chair, raised one eyebrow, and looked at me. No, he studied me. Not in a threatening way but with curiosity. After what seemed like ten minutes — which was really only a few seconds — he slid the paper back over to himself, wrote the word SYSTEMS in large letters at the top, and slid it back to me, still with that curious look on his face.

"Okay, okay," I was exasperated but amused that I had even tried. "If I cannot write it in the form of a system, I cannot delegate it, and I will forever be handcuffed to it. Strike what I said before; it was more of an excuse for why I don't have job descriptions than a real answer anyway. I recognize that now. No more excuses. I promise."

"Make that promise to yourself, Ruben, not to me." He paused long enough for that to sink in before he continued, "So if you did have job descriptions, they would define the primary duties associated with the position, and under each primary duty, would be a list of responsibilities associated with that primary duty. Also, for each primary duty, there would be a method of measurement."

Inside the circle I wrote:

> Primary duty
>
> > a. Responsibility
> >
> > b. Responsibility
> >
> > c. Responsibility
>
> Method of Measurement

"Very good. Now, in the upper left of the job descriptions, draw another circle and label it Recruiting and Interviewing; to the right of that, another labeled Hiring, Orientation & Training; south of that, on the bottom right, another circle labeled Performance Evaluation; to the left of that, another labeled Career Advancement. Now, connect all of the exterior circles with arrows, starting from the upper right."

Coach watched as I drew the diagram according to his instruction. I couldn't help but feel like a school kid who hadn't done his homework and was now being made to finish the assignment in front of the teacher.

"Good. Finally, draw a two-way arrow from the center circle, the Job Description, to each exterior circle. Now, what does that diagram tell you?"

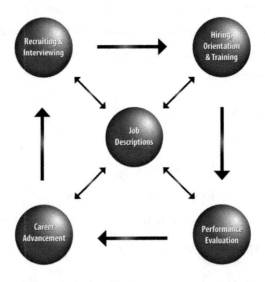

Somehow it all magically came together.

In order to get maximum performance, I must recruit, hire, train, evaluate, and promote people based on how well they perform the established jobs.

"This diagram tells me that I have been doing HR wrong since we started the company. I have always hired from the perceived need for another position and always from the gut. I now know why we struggle with performance evaluations; we struggle because they are not tied back to anything concrete."

And I thought this Administration stuff was going to be boring. I was so wrong. This element is a game-changer for my business!

"Okay, I am a 1 on this element. Let's get to the next element." I was so eager to learn more. I was soaking his stuff up like a sponge! I had pages and pages of notes.

More, more, more… Feed me! I feel like that oversized plant named Audrey 2 in the musical Little Shop of Horrors*…the one that gobbles up everything!*

"Well then, let's get to the next Discipline before you lose interest in this *boring* Discipline."

I knew it! He reads minds! How else does he know what I'm thinking?

"Tell me about the next element," he prompted.

I looked down at the chart and said it out loud, "Communication. Well, I can assume this means that the systems one has in place to manage Communications with employees. As with HR, we have no systems for Communications at my company, other than our frequent 'hallway huddles' or our 'coffee and cooler conferences.'"

Coach sat back in his chair and gave me that curious look again.

"We actually call them that, Coach. For years, we have said that we don't need no stinking meetings because our 'hallway huddles' and 'coffee and cooler conferences' were enough."

Coach just sat there, staring at me, but this time, he let his amusement show. "That is one form of communication. However, when we think systems and communication, we think of structured communication. So, can you give me some examples of structured communication in business?"

"Yes," I quickly replied. "The newly implemented coaching sessions with my key people is an example of structured communication."

"Exactly. Can you write a system on frequency, agenda, and conduct for an effective coaching session, a system that future managers can use to ensure consistency of coaching for your organization?"

"Yes, I can clearly see that. Are there more ways to build systems in this element?"

"Can you think of anymore?"

Why is he always reversing questions on me? Does he think it's possible that I'm not thinking hard enough here?

"Well, we could have monthly staff meetings to discuss the implementation of new systems as we learn about them. Also, I could send out a monthly message to the whole company that summarizes organizational improvements, CSI status, and new systems that we will be working on in the current month."

Here comes that excitement again!

"Very good. So far, all of your communication system examples are internal. What about your customers, vendors, or community at large?"

—⟊⟊⟊—

"Coach, are these elements independent of each other, or do they often interface?"

—⟊⟊⟊—

"Well, if we do the Customer Feedback Interviews, that would be structured communication with our clients, and if we do a monthly e-blast to our database to further our visibility, build credibility, and demonstrate ability, that would be structured communication for the community at large."

Something was beginning to happen. Somehow these systems were beginning to touch each other, if not interlock directly. "Coach, are these elements independent of each other, or do they often interface?"

"What would be more efficient? If they were independent, or if they interfaced?"

"Well, obviously, if they interfaced."

"Great, now think of your growing company. Do you want departmental cyclones or do you want one organization that interfaces at all levels?"

It all started to clear up at that exact moment. Although we were assessing my business by element, it was clear that our objective was to create systems that linked together, thus bonding every employee in every department together. It was so clear, yet so confusing at the same time.

"Okay, I think I have a handle on what is happening to me. It seems that we want to intentionally interface these elements, so as to create one BIG system where every job and department interacts with each other. Is that correct?"

"You are getting it. How would you rate yourself on the element of Communications?"

"1." I said it matter-of-factly. I no longer cringed when offering a low number.

I now know I have the power to improve any part of my business.

"Move on?"

"Move on." I confirmed and looked down at the chart.

"Coach, before you ask, the next element is Calendar and

Scheduling, and we all use outlook at my company. Outlook is a pretty good calendaring system?" I was reaching and I knew it.

"I agree. Outlook is a great calendaring tool; in fact, most of our clients use Outlook. Beyond Outlook, what else comes to mind when you think Calendaring and Scheduling as a system?"

"Other than having access to see my employees' calendars, I can't think of anything else. Can you help me out here?" I was struggling to see where this could be a system for business.

He/she who manages the calendar manages the business.

"I am going to tell you another CEO Rule, and I want you to tell me what you think it means. 'He/she who manages the calendar manages the business.' Now, what does that mean to you, Ruben?" He watched and waited for my answer.

"Well, I guess it means that if I want myself and my people to get certain things done, then they should be on a calendar. Is that right?"

Somehow I know there is more.

"Close, very close. Think of your Finance department. Can you think of ten things that are operation critical and must be done every month?"

I was beginning to see where he was going with this. "Yes, payroll needs to be submitted on the twenty-fifth and the tenth of each month in order to meet payroll on the first and fifteenth. Also, certain reports need to be generated at the beginning of the month, and bank reconciliation has to happen every month."

"Do these things get done every month at the frequency that you expect, and are there other financial activities that must happen every month?"

"Honestly, I am always on my Accounting manager's back to get me the financial reports on time for my meeting with our bankers. Also, we have come very close to missing payroll due to late submissions. As for more activities, yes, there are many more, but what is the sense if they are struggling to get these few things done?" I struggled to keep the desperation out of my voice.

Coach moved on quickly. "Let's say you and your Accounting manager met during a coaching session to lay out a standard monthly Finance calendar that had specific recurring dates each month on which specific activities had to be completed. And let's say that there was an understanding that you were to be notified two days prior if the manager knew he/she would not meet the scheduled date. How could you use this calendar to better lead your Accounting manager? What if you had a like calendar for your Sales/Marketing manager?" He leaned forward, emphatically tapping his pointer finger on his desk. "In fact, what if every manager in your company had a published calendar of operation critical recurring calendared activities? How would this help you, and how would it help them?"

Ouch, this is so obvious. How could I have missed it?

"If we had these departmental calendars, we would reduce a lot of frustration and confusion as to when key activities are to be completed. My Production manager would not have to wonder when he was going to get his departmental expense report; my IT department would not have to worry about when the next marketing flyer was to be sent out, and so on, and so on. Is this what you were referring to when you mentioned efficiency earlier?" This was such a basic, but key element of business; in fact, it seemed like every element was basic and key.

How am I going to determine where to start?

"Rating?"

"1, but that will change."

Darn right, it will.

"Next element?"

My mind was spinning with the possibilities to greatly improve my business via the Core Disciplines of Business. And, to top it off, none of this stuff seemed really difficult.

Could I be missing something?

"The next element, and the last element in Administration, is General Office. What I know about General Office is what I felt fully described the Discipline of Administration when we started: the receptionist, the office manager, and the filing." Part of me wanted to ask, "What more could there be?" but I had come to know better.

Coach slid another blank piece of paper to me, and I had a pretty good idea as to what was coming next.

"What do you want me to draw?" I was not being sarcastic. I was eager to see what he wanted me to draw. In fact, every one of these drawings was going home with me, and I was going to put them in a coaching binder.

"Let me ask you a few questions regarding this element. First of all, are you tracking the volume and nature of all incoming calls to your company? For those that are urgent or critical regarding a customer, vendor, regulatory agency, or employee, are you managing those calls for prompt resolution?"

"Other than documenting and managing customer complaints, no."

I was not quite sure where Coach was going with this.

"Okay, let's say that over a one-month period you logged 300 phone calls and 80% were customer complaints. What would that tell you? Or, 50% were employees inquiring about benefits? Or 40% were vendors inquiring about payment? Tracking the volume of calls and the nature of calls tells quite a story of what may be going on in the business. And, more importantly, tracking reveals the areas for significant improvement in service to customers, vendors, or employees. Can you see this?"

"Well, yes. If I knew that even 40% of our calls were employees inquiring about benefits, we could hold meetings to review the employee handbook and benefit programs. If I saw that 40% were vendors inquiring about payment, I could meet with my Accounting manager and see what was happening." That had happened not too long ago. My Accounting manager made the decision not to use the line of credit and stretch out vendor payments to make payroll. I found out about it when my most important vendor wanted to put us on a cash basis.

Man, was I angry! And I took all of that anger home. That was a bad night. That was a bad night. Actually, that whole week was awful.

"Very good. Now think of a similar system for tracking incoming mail. I have found many of our clients scanning all incoming mail that is not trash, then filing and forwarding the scanned document to the appropriate party. If it is a bill, it goes to Accounting. If a sales inquiry, it goes to the Sales manager, and so on," he said. "This scanning and filing eliminates the need for photo copies and completely does away with the management of paper distribution. Also, reports can be generated to tell you the volume of incoming mail and to whom it was sent. How would this benefit you?"

"Well, Accounting would get information much faster. As it is now, the mail is sent upstairs to Accounting once per week. And

———⟜∾∾⟞———

This is where I would put all of the corporate documents when I get my systems in place!

———⟜∾∾⟞———

the other managers pick up their mail at no regular frequency. If the document was emailed to them then placed in an electronic folder, we would be much faster at responding to mailed inquiries." I paused, seeing it all unfold in my mind. "I like this very much, especially since the office is making a copy of everything they are distributing due to a history of 'I never got that mail' syndrome. This could be huge for us."

"I am excited to see you so excited about General Office. I am sure there are other types of information that flow through your company, but for now, I think you get the point. The other function of General Office is to function as the company's document repository. All corporate documents should be managed here," he paused, moving his gaze from the chart back to me. "Tell me, what are some types of documents that are important to manage?"

"Well, there are sales collateral, all of the job descriptions — when I have developed them — and performance evaluations, training materials, employee handbooks, and the benefits summary."

This is where I would put all of the corporate documents when I get my systems in place!

"How do you manage these documents now, and how certain are you that your team is using the current version?"

"I am not."

Hey, I could put this online as well. Why keep hard copies of all these? Let's scan in the most current version and use that as the repository.

"I can see your mind working already." Coach looked pleased. "Now, the last key role of General Office is the management of all regulatory licenses, renewals, and all company administrative user IDs/passwords. Tell me how you manage this now."

I shook my head. "We are always getting surprised by an expired license or cannot find a user ID/password when we need it. That is very frustrating."

I don't even want to know how much time I waste looking for passwords — or changing them because no one can find them!

"Sounds to me that you have some work to do here as well," he looked at me pointedly. "Tell me, what do you know about General Office now?" Coach smiled.

"I know that we need to start tracking incoming calls and scanning incoming mail. We need to set up a corporate document repository and make a master list of all license renewals. We also need to have one place where we keep all company user ids/passwords."

Whew, that is a lot! I looked back down at the blank piece of paper Coach had put in front of me, and it was full, on both sides, with notes. Is there any part of the business the Coach has no systems for? Forget I asked that.

"Coach, I must admit, I thought that Administration was going to be a boring topic. I had no idea how important this Discipline really is and how many systems in Administration touch the other Disciplines."

"As I said earlier, Administration is the glue that holds the business together. Can you see that now?"

"Absolutely! And I give myself a 1 here as well. That gives me a whopping 4 out of 15 for this Discipline. No worries though, I will get this one up to speed fast."

Here I am again, thinking that all of these are so simple that I can just implement them tomorrow. Coach warned me of this, and I am sure he warned me for a reason.

This time, when we finished Administration, we wasted no time. We went directly into the next Discipline of Operations.

Oh boy, this looks like a scary one!

THE FIFTH DISCIPLINE

OPERATIONS

*"It is not total sales, but gross profit
that pays the bills..."*

~ Coach ~

It is amazing how comfortable I feel with Coach. No doubt, I am on the edge of my comfort zone, but somehow, he makes it okay to not know what I don't know. I don't know how he does it, but I don't know if the "how" matters. I'm just grateful to be here with him.

I looked around the room again, taking in all of the detail that I had come to believe was deliberate, while Coach poured himself another cold drink.

The desk, the chess table…he does it all with intention. I'm sure of it.

"I can't help but notice that large sixty-minute clock you have on your desk." I gestured in the direction of the clock.

Coach had an 8-inch by 8-inch white-faced clock, in the left corner of his desk. In place of the normal hour numbers around the face were the numbers 0 through 60, in ten-minute increments. As time passed, the white turned to red. I noticed that because the previously white face was now almost completely red. It looked like we had about four minutes left in this hour.

This tool helps me, and the client, to stay on schedule.

Coach waited for me to ask the question.

"Would you tell me how you use that?"

"Sure, my normal scheduled coaching sessions with a client or team member are for one hour. This tool helps me, and the client, to stay on schedule," Coach replied.

"How is that?"

"Let me ask you: Why did you think to inquire about the timer?"

Again, another question to get me to think about my own question.

"It is kind of hard to ignore it with the face turning red as time passes. Ahh…it's a timer, right?"

I think my own face was beginning to match the clock's.

"Yes, there is something about the face turning from white to red that calls the attention of the client at a conscious or subconscious level. In every coaching session, the timer is placed in the middle of the table after being set for one hour. In our case, I will reset it after the first hour, and the white face will begin to turn red all over again."

What a brilliant way to keep people on schedule. There is no need to tell people you are running out of time because the timer tells them that. I mean, it is really hard to ignore this huge white face turning red as time passes.

"Is there an alarm?"

"There is, should you turn the sound on. However, I have found it to be very effective without the sound." Coached picked up the clock and spun the red dial back to 0 showing the all-white face again.

I felt relief. I had more time to spend with Coach.

I really hope I have much more time. I have to implement this stuff.

I sensed an urgency that I hadn't felt before.

"This must mean we only have an hour left. So should we get started?" I was eager to learn how much I don't know about Operations.

What a different outlook from my first few Disciplines.

"Sure, tell me what you know about Operations."

Coach began every Discipline the same way. First, he wanted to know how much I knew about the Discipline before getting into each element of it. It did not take me long to catch onto this pattern. I recognized it after the second Discipline, expected it on the third, and fell into the pattern by the fourth.

What an excellent way to help people learn. First, assess what they know, then fill in the gaps based on your knowledge. I must begin doing this with my employees and managers, as this is very different from the normal "sit down and let me tell you everything you need to know about X" approach that I have used in the past.

"Operations. Well, when I think of Operations, I think of my Production department and all that it takes for us to make, assemble, and ship our products. That would include everything from facilities and equipment maintenance, purchasing and inventory management, to production scheduling and shipping." I felt pretty good about this part of my business because I had spent eight years as a Production manager for my previous employer.

Coach nodded his approval. "That is pretty good — so good that I need not add anything to your answer. Let's move on to the first element in Operations."

As with the beginning of each Discipline, Coach started each element by asking me to explain the systems I had in place for each element.

How is it that I, the founder, owner, and CEO of the company, cannot quantify how we systematically performed these key elements of business? One by one, I will get these systems in place.

"The first element is Quality. Now, I feel like we put out a good quality product, but cannot really tell you what system we have in place for this. We did look at some of the ISO Quality programs, but found them to be cumbersome and expensive, especially since none of our clients require that level of certification. The last time we investigated that, it was going to cost us over \$250,000 to fully implement. So, to answer the direct question, I must say we have no formal Quality systems in place."

Ouch, that hurt. But it is the truth. How is it that I, the founder, owner, and CEO of the company, cannot quantify how we systematically performed these key elements of business? One by one, I will get these systems in place.

"You are proving, over and over again, to be an honest man, Ruben. I appreciate that." Coach's voice and expression were sincere.

"Thanks. I am beginning to understand that if I am to improve, I must take a hard and truthful look at my company. And, you make it kind of easy to be honest."

That was true. If I were to lie and tell Coach, *"Yeah, I have a good Quality system in place,"* he would hand me a blank sheet of paper and ask me to draw it out. I learned that lesson the hard way.

No, there is no lying to Coach.

"How do you mean, Ruben?"

"Well, it seems that every time I am not completely honest, you find a way to catch me in a lie."

"Do you feel it is my goal to catch you in a lie?" He smiled, obviously genuinely interested in this line of conversation.

"Well, kind of. I remember how it felt the last time you made me prove a system I really did not have." I was not quite sure where this was going, but I opened the door to this dialogue and was waiting, almost in anticipation, to see where it went. As with everything Coach did and said, I was sure there was a lesson to be learned here.

"What could I possibly gain by catching you in a lie? And what could I really do about it if I did?"

"Good point. You really have nothing to gain by catching me in a lie."

"So, if my motivation is *not* to catch you in a lie, then what *is* my motivation?"

Here it comes.

I took a deep breath before answering. "Well, I guess your only other motivation would be to help me stay honest because, as you said early on, you can only help me if I am honest with you."

There it was. The golden nugget of this dialogue: My motivation should never be to catch my people in a lie. My sole motivation should be to help them stay honest.

"You've got it. Now, tell me the difference between the two motivations."

I shifted in my seat and suddenly realized that my entire body was leaning forward, as if trying to get a closer look at an amazing image. Leaning back in my chair, I took a few seconds to really think about this reply.

"Well, if my motivation is to catch people in a lie, then the outcome of those conversations would be consequences, or punishment, and people would eventually begin to clam up when talking with me."

Is that why my Production manager only gave me one-word answers to my questions in our last meeting? Could I have caused that behavior by my leadership style?

Coach leaned forward and brought me back to the conversation.

"On the other hand, if my motivation is to help people stay honest, then the outcome would be lessons learned, and I can truly help them to improve while maintaining an open dialogue."

Somewhere in that answer was my true lesson.

"If my people do not trust me enough to remain open and honest with me, then I will get to a point where I can no longer help them."

There is the lesson! I cannot fully help people who are not open and honest with me!

Could I have caused that behavior by my leadership style?

"And what are the consequences of that?" Coach drilled down even further.

"They will either underperform and get fired, or they will quit." The moment I said that, all of the faces of the good employees I had lost over the past year came flooding back into my thoughts.

Coach must have sensed my mind beginning to wander. "What are you thinking, Ruben?"

"I was thinking about all the key people I lost this past year and wondering if I had chased them away." Feeling the weight of my responsibility, I hung my head.

"Great question; however, one that will never be answered. All we can do is change the way we do things in the future if we want a different result."

I know I chased them away, but he's right, I don't have to do that again.

I smiled, looked up at Coach, and said, "You sure do have a way of making me feel better."

"What would I gain would I gain by making you feel bad?" Coach asked. His voice suddenly had a fatherly tone to it.

I stepped right into that one.

"You would not gain by making me feel bad, Coach. In fact, I would imagine that many of your clients look forward to coaching sessions with you largely because you make them feel good. I would."

My people dread meetings with me; they leave my office with their head down and feeling bad.

I looked at the large timer on Coach's desk and seven minutes were red. Coach saw me look at the clock and picked up on my cue. "I can see that you are concerned about the time."

"Yeah, don't we need to complete the evaluation?"

"We will, but keep in mind that a huge part of my job is to identify what I call 'Coaching Moments.' Often, the most impactful lessons learned come from conversation not on the agenda, and I would be making a critical professional error to force our agenda and miss those moments. Here is the rule: 'The best lessons learned are caught, not taught.' Can you tell me what that means?"

The best lessons learned are caught, not taught. Wow.

"That means that I have to put my agenda aside when meeting with my people, focus on what they say, and try to help them catch their lessons."

> *The best lessons learned are caught, not taught.*

That's going to be tough to do!

"You have got it, Ruben. You are a quick study! I will give you that." He smiled, confirming his pleasure in my understanding of these concepts. "Now let's discuss Quality systems."

"I'm ready." I took a deep breath and readied myself to catch the next lesson.

"If you were to define Quality as a form of measurement, Ruben, what would you measure?"

Wow, now that is a question I have never considered.

"I would either measure customer complaints or number of rejects."

I recalled a recent meeting with my Customer Service team when our volume of customer complaints increased where I told them, "Every company has problems. What sets the good companies apart from the bad is how they respond to those problems."

"Good things to measure, but are those measurements of Quality or of Non-Quality?"

*Hmmmmm...*I took my time before answering.

"I guess those would both be measurements of Non-Quality, if there were such a term. I am at a loss here, Coach." I was struggling to come up with some simple measures of Quality versus Non-Quality.

"Let's go back to the 'all work is a process' discussion. Do you recall that?"

"Yes, we applied that rule to the Sales Process, then again in Human Resources, and quite frankly, it applies to almost every element."

"That is correct. Can you figure out how it may apply here?"

"Sure. Since Production is all about moving work through the building, physically, then designing a master 'workflow' would fit quite nice."

Not quite sure where this is heading yet.

"Good start. Now, expand your image of Operations beyond just Production, and picture your entire operation. Now apply what you just said."

Ahhh…I see where this is going.

"Well, under those terms, I would have to map out my entire business on a master flow chart. Everything from how leads are generated to final shipping, invoicing, and collections." My chest tightened as I imagined the amount of time and energy it would take to map my entire operation. "That's a huge job, Coach."

—◈—

"I agree. This is a huge undertaking and would require several days in a meeting room with the walls lined with butcher block paper and your key management team involved," he said, leaning forward with his elbows on his desk. "But, let's suppose we have this planning session with your leaders and begin mapping out your entire operation's work flow. What would it look like?"

My chest tightened as I imagined the amount of time and energy it would take to map my entire operation. "That's a huge job, Coach."

"Well, I would imagine a bunch of circles representing steps in our workflow with arrows directing work through the Operations. Am I

—◈—

on track?" I had the mental image but was struggling to fit this into a Quality system.

"Great. Now explain to me how a sales order gets submitted in your company," he prompted, taking my thoughts deeper.

"Well, if it is an inside sales person who is taking orders from existing customers, they fill out the order form and submit it to

Customer Service where the order is processed and materials are purchased."

"Excellent. On this blank sheet of paper, draw two circles and label one Sales Order and the other Order Processing. Now, think of only the Order Processing circle and make a list of all the information needed to have a "Quality" order — an order that will sail smoothly through this circle."

Inside the circle, I began to write my list:

1. Approved pricing
2. Gross profit calculations
3. Product dimensions
4. Product description from standard cost or client profile
5. Product quantity
6. Customer signed order form

When I completed my list, I handed the paper back to Coach.

He read over the list, carefully, taking his time before responding. "Great. Now I am sure there is more to this list that you and I cannot think of, but let's assume this list is complete, and let's call this list a Quality Checklist. If that were the case, how could you use this Quality Checklist?"

"Well, I could give it to my sales people, and they could use it when submitting a new order to ensure it is complete and accurate. I can also track and measure the number of times an order was inaccurate or incomplete, what information was missing, and who the submitting sales rep was. We could then use that tracking to fix orders upon submission, before we purchase any product, and also to identify training needs for the Sales department."

Wow. This little checklist could save us some enormous headaches!

My pulse raced with the possibilities.

"Outstanding! Now, if we look at your two circles, and were to redefine who we call the Internal Customer and Internal Vendor in this relationship, who would be the Customer and who would be the Vendor, and what is the Product?"

"The Internal Customer would be order processing, the Internal Vendor would be the Sales department, and the Product would be the sales order." It was getting much clearer. "And if the checklist became the Quality standard, and every order met the Quality standards of order processing (the internal customer), we would have no new order submission errors."

144 | Know Your Next Move: The 7 Core Disciplines of Business

There is the answer. Quality is the process of identifying the entire organizational workflow, establishing internal customer/vendor relationships, determining the internal customer standards for Quality, and using measurement to correct errors along the process, and for training. If we were to do this successfully, the number of customer complaints would drop considerably, the number of re-orders would diminish, and thousands of dollars would fall to the bottom line! How could I have missed this? I have to schedule this planning meeting soon! There I go again, wanting to get everything done next week. Slow down, Ruben. This is a marathon, not a sprint!

—*ᔕᔕᔕ*—

Quality is the process of identifying the entire organizational work flow, establishing internal customer/ vendor relationships, determining the internal customer standards for Quality, and using measurement to correct errors along the process, and for training.

—*ᔕᔕᔕ*—

"I love your enthusiasm; however, I get the sense that you want to head right back to your office, pull your team together, and have this Workflow Process planning session tomorrow. Is that correct?" There was caution in his voice.

There he goes — reading my mind again.

"Actually, that is exactly what I was thinking. But I know that is not the intent of this session. Our goal is to create the awareness. However, how am I going to know which one to start with? How do I figure out the next move? I mean, it seems like I need to do all of these ASAP!" My voice sounded as strained as my brain felt.

"Trust the process," was all Coach said.

"Before we leave this element, I do have a question for you. How do you see this element touching Administration and Human Resources?"

"I can see steps in the workflow process as part of the employee's job descriptions and training schedule," I replied confidently.

"Per-*fec*-to!" Coach exclaimed. "May I tell you a quick story?" He looked like he was considering sharing a secret.

"Of course!" I leaned forward again.

"Recently, we worked with a client to complete his first organizational workflow process. They did such a great job with it that they had it painted along three walls in their large employee break room. What benefits do you see them gaining from that large drawing of the workflow?"

I was getting used to his turning the tables, and shooting a question at me.

"I would imagine that it would help each employee to visually see where they fit into the bigger picture and how errors they make could affect the entire workflow. It could be used for training purposes, elimination of redundancies, and clarity of work duties. It would also help employees see how their co-workers fit into the big picture. I am sure there are more, but…" My voice trailed off with my thoughts.

Our oversized conference/employee break room would be perfect for this. We could take the outdated pictures down and replace them with a large diagram of our entire organizational workflow.

"Exactly. Ruben, here are two rules to remember: Rule #1: 'If your employees cannot describe their job as a process, then they don't know their job.' Rule #2: 'If the business owner cannot describe his/her company as a process, then he/she does not know their business.'"

Ouch!

"Okay, Coach, I got it. I am going to rate myself as a 1 here, but not for long."

Coach chuckled. "Next element."

"The next element in the Discipline of Operations is Systems Process. Before you ask, let me tell you what this means to me. Before our discussion about Quality, I would not have had much to say about this element, but knowing what I know now, I would say that this element is all about documenting specific processes." I sat up in my chair, excited to learn.

"You are on the right track!" Coach confirmed. "Now, describe for me the documentation and how you would use it?"

"Well, I would take each step in the workflow process and have the employees write a simple "Step 1, Step 2, Step 3" Standard Operating Procedure (SOP) for each and then put them into a departmental operations manual. Then I could use these SOPs for performance reviews, initial training, cross training, and to accompany a job description. As positions change, I would shift SOPs around, and as the business changes, we can use these SOPs to manage that change. We can also use these SOPs for internal audits to ensure we are consistent with our work output." There was so much running through my mind, the relationship between all of the elements, and the potential significant enhancement to my business was mind blowing!

If your employees cannot describe their job as a process, then they don't know their job.

"You are definitely a process thinker! Rating?"

"I am currently at a 1 here as well, but I see the close relationship between Quality and Process and can imagine them both moving up concurrently in the ratings."

"I agree. I think you have a pretty good sense of Process, so let's move on to the next element in Operations." With Coach, there was no wasting time.

I was clearly in rhythm with this process. "The next element is Productive Labor (Production Standards) and, if I were to guess, I would assume that this element has something to do with making labor productive?"

"Clever, Ruben, but can you be a bit more specific?"

"Actually, I was not being clever at all. I don't quite know how this would be different from what we already discussed." For some reason, my mind went blank.

And I was on such a roll!

"Okay, let me help you out a bit." Once again, he paused, making sure he had my complete attention. "Are you familiar with the term Productive Labor?"

"Probably not to the extent that I should be, as has proven to be the case with almost every element. If I were to take a stab at it, I would assume that this element has systems that ensure your Productive Labor is tracked against some established targets. Am I on track?"

"Not only are you on track — you are spot on." He took a sip of his water, reminding me that I hadn't touched my own. I took a swig as he continued, "Let me back up a bit and briefly describe how labor breaks down in most businesses. In business, there are three types of labor — one being Revenue Generating. Can you tell me who those people are in your company?"

"Sure, these are my sales guys and, partially, my field service team who can make additional sales in the field."

"Beautiful. Now, do you have sales quotas or goals for them to reach each month?"

"Yes, we are a sales organization. We have weekly sales meetings where the sales people post their numbers, and we provide product, skill, or industry/company knowledge training during those meetings." I felt pretty confident here.

—*ᘒᘒᘒ*—

In business, there are three types of labor.

—*ᘒᘒᘒ*—

"Great, another type of labor is Administrative and Management. Tell me about how you treat/monitor this group differently." He wasn't letting up.

"Well, this group is composed of the leaders of the company. When we meet, we discuss bigger picture strategy and goals. Other than overall departmental performance, we do not set the same types of goals for this group. Nonetheless, we do set goals for them." I felt good about this answer.

"Very good. The third type of labor in any company, regardless of whether the company is in home mortgage lending, or manufacturing, is called Productive Labor. It is this labor pool that gets the work done and out the door," Coach explained. "Can you tell me about your Productive Labor team and how you manage them?"

I was beginning to wonder where Coach was going with this one. "Yeah, this is our Production team, and we track whether or not we hit our shipping numbers for the day by department." There was a little doubt overshadowing my earlier confidence. I began to feel like an emotional yo-yo in this process again.

"Excellent. Now think back to the employee doing the work. Does each employee have a piece per hour standard or something equivalent?"

"Well, not that finite."

He got me on this one.

"How does the employee know if he/she is succeeding in their job? Also, and more importantly, how do you know if you are properly staffed? Let's say the Production backlog requires you to put out 200,000 units in the next ten days. If we had a standard of 10,000 units per day per person, how many people would we need?"

"Looks like only two."

"Exactly. Now tell me how establishing Production Standards for unit output for each position in Production can help you."

Knowing that I would eventually get this, as I did with all of the other elements, I dove into my explanation. "Well, it would help me to greatly control my Productive Labor cost and have a real way of measuring what labor is needed against what is scheduled to ship. This can help immensely with better managing our labor cost, which has been a challenge for us. We always seem to go over in production due to labor. I can see us setting up Production Standards for every unit on the floor." My excitement returned.

Coach nodded, and I continued: "This could be huge for scheduling and planning what employees need to be doing each day! And we can build some employee recognition programs around exceeding standards. This could be very cool, but I do see where it will take quite some time and effort to put this all together."

"As with many of the elements, it will take a team to properly understand the goal of the system, develop the system, implement the system, monitor the system, and ultimately trust the system," he paused to let this settle in. "But what are the longer term gains for you, the company, and the employee?"

"Well, the employees will clearly know exactly what is expected of them and their output on any given day. That alone is huge. Production management can better plan the use of labor based on the volume of work, not the number of employees he has to put to work, and the company gains much better control of the Productive Labor costs."

Alleluia!

"So, how would you rate Productive Labor for your company now?"

"We are at a 2 and need to begin building time studies on the output of every unit on the floor, one unit at a time, and then begin to use that as a standard for our productive labor team. Sounds pretty black and white for me." It really did.

I can visualize a report where my Production manager sends me his labor plan based on unit output versus just dollars.

I noticed the red on the clock was half full, indicating that we only had thirty minutes left to finish this assessment. "We do not have much time left, yet we still need to complete Operations, only one left, and then assess IT and Finance. What happens if we do not finish?"

"Great question, but I think you already know whether or not you want to become a client based on what has already been assessed. Finishing is ideal; however, the primary goal is to help you realize that you don't know what you don't know, and then to create an opportunity for you to succeed. We will get as far as we can, and then you will tell me what you want to do moving forward. Fair enough?"

"Yes, Sir." Coach had information I needed, and I was committed to getting it.

Yes, if Coach were to ask me to make a decision at this moment, I would say, "I'm all in" enthusiastically. Hmm…I wonder why he has not tried to close the deal?

"Let's finish the last element in Operations and move to IT. So, tell me what you know about Materials Management. Remember, I want to know about *your* systems for Materials Management," he nodded at me, waiting for my explanation.

"Here is where it can easily get way out of control. If we have one job go bad due to poor material pricing or, worse yet, wrong material purchases, we lose money on the job. I have seen months where labor came in on budget at 26% while material came in at 45%, leaving me only 29% gross profit. Our target GP is 40% and two or three of those kinds of months can kill our year."

I never quite understood how we could so grossly miscalculate material costs to the extent that we lose money on a job.

"Not uncommon, but tell me about your systems to control Materials."

"Other than watching over the shoulder of our Purchasing agent for every purchase to ensure they are purchasing the correct material at the right price, I don't know what kind of system to put in place."

Here comes the frustration again. I could feel it in my throat this time. *I never quite understood how we could so grossly miscalculate material costs to the extent that we lose money on a job.* That totally burned my chops, and I let Production know it. Just last month, I had to tell my wife we lost $200K due to poor material purchasing for the month, and we were not going to recover a single penny from that. *Whew! She was as mad as I was!* Thinking of this added to the sinking feeling in the pit of my stomach.

"I sense that this topic gives you some anxiety. Am I correct?" He looked concerned.

"Very much so. We work too hard to secure and serve our clients, only to lose money due to incompetent purchasing. That is unacceptable!" The rage that came up shouldn't have surprised me, but I looked away from Coach. "This isn't just about business, Coach. All of this is putting a serious strain on my marriage." I looked down when my voice cracked.

"I'm sorry to hear that, Ruben. I see business owners in this situation often. It does take its toll on one's personal life, especially the marriages. Let's see if we can smooth out your systems and alleviate some of that pressure at work *and* at home."

"Thank you, Coach."

Coach stood up and signaled for me to join him at the table with the chessboard, probably in an effort to move me out of the physical and emotional space I had just been in so I could think about systems again.

"What are the key components of a sound system?"

"Well, they are written down and proven, they have predictable results and can be measured, and most importantly, they can be easily monitored."

"Very good. Now tell me, how many checks and balances do you have on your office manager to ensure your cash gets to the bank?"

"Many. Without cash, we are out of business."

"And if you allowed your office manager to make $200,000 cash use decisions with your checking account, what types of controls would you put in place to ensure the use of cash was 100% correct and approved by you?" He was drilling down again.

"First of all, that would never happen, but I am beginning to see your point. I am not treating purchasing with the same intensity and carefulness as I treat my cash."

"Your Purchasing agent is spending your cash at the rate of hundreds of thousands of dollars per day with more freedom than you have as the owner." Coach's intensity surprised me. I could tell he was genuinely concerned. "So, let's go back to the idea that 'all work is a process,' and see if we can quickly map out the hot spots for your Purchasing process that may need to be monitored, verified, or even approved prior to purchasing anything. You take the lead and draw out a simple workflow for Purchasing only and highlight the key areas where increased monitoring, verification, or approval should be implemented."

I took a few minutes to draw out the workflow process as Coach watched patiently from his side of the table. Then I turned the paper so we could both view it.

"Well, the first thing would be to ensure the Purchasing and Sales teams meet to go over every piece of materials requested by the customer and to ensure the customer's signature is on the Materials order form. Wait a minute!" The AHA hit me with force. "We don't have a separate Materials order form the customer signs off on. We need to implement this ASAP. Okay, after that, we need to get three quotes for each material on the list with the goal of purchasing less than our target. At this point, I would like to see a Material Purchase master list for the job that shows what we estimated, our actual cost per our Purchase Order, with the Vendor and the calculated Gross Profits."

Unlike some of the other elements we have talked about waiting to implement, this is important for you to implement now.

I must be on to something. Coach looks pleased!

"Finally, I would want to pay 100% from our purchase orders, not the vendors' invoices. If the vendor approves the PO, then they should accept payment from that PO. If I had these simple approvals in place per job, then I would feel much more comfortable and in control of our Purchasing system."

"Amazing! You laid it all out so simply in five minutes; why have you not implemented this at work?" Coach gently prodded.

I had no answer, and I sat there searching for it for what seemed like an eternity. "Why did I not come up with this system and implement it before I met you?" I shook my head. "I have no idea."

"Unlike some of the other elements we have talked about waiting to implement, this is important for you to implement now. Realize, however, that this will require fairly significant oversight up front until it really becomes the way your Purchasing department does business. That oversight must come from whom?"

"Me, of course."

"If you take full management, oversight, and monitoring control, what happens to your Production manager's relationship with his/her purchasing manager?"

Hmmm…I wonder how long it would have taken me to think about this on my own.

Taking another deep breath, I continued, "I need to review the system and decide at what points I want to be informed and/or need to approve purchases. That could have been a huge mistake. In fact, I cannot be the one to implement this system. I need to train my Production manager and let him implement the system. Thanks, Coach. That could have really messed me up."

Man, I need to quit doing that. I remembered what had happened the last time I had made a quick decision like this. My boy had an issue with another student, and I immediately went to the teacher to get it resolved, not considering how that would affect my son's reputation at school. *The problem is solved, but he is still paying the price for my rash decision-making, and he is still mad as all get out at me.*

"Where are we on the rating for Operations?"

"I think I am at 4 out of 5 again, but I may be off a few points. Regardless, this one is going to take a lot of work to get fully implemented."

"Coach, do businesses owners realistically implement all of these systems in two years?" I suddenly felt myself sinking under the pressure of all the work that lay ahead.

Coach shrugged his shoulders. "That depends on several factors. First, it depends on the size of the company and whether they have the resources in house to develop and implement. The Culture of execution is huge; some companies talk a great game of improvement and yet struggle to get things started and completed. Most importantly, the owner's willingness to let go and drive these changes throughout the organization is key. Your people are amazing, with incredible capacity, given the opportunity to demonstrate it. Most owners are surprised at how much more their people can get done. I am sure there are other factors, but in my experience, those seem to be the most common. Now, having said that, I have clients who have been through the CEO Club multiple times; some have repeated the program up to five times. Why do you think that is?"

"I would think that after a two-year session, you would graduate and move on."

"That would seem obvious, however, as our clients mature into their new roles of less 'doing the doing' and more CEO work of delegating and supporting, their perspective of each element changes. And when they attend class, they hear the content with a different set of filters, and the content appears as if it were rewritten and refreshed just for them. My history is that 89% of my clients renewed for a subsequent two years and then either remain in the CEO Club or move up to the Chairman's Club. Besides, they have been meeting side-by-side with a peer group for two years. Who would want to leave such a trusted resource?"

We believe improvement never ends, and as a result, we are always learning new business and leadership strategies that we either incorporate into our curriculum or just share with our clients.

"So you are saying I may never graduate?" This sounded more like a marriage commitment than a coaching relationship. And I wasn't doing so well in the marriage department lately.

"What I am saying is that you will decide when you feel you know it all and no longer need our help. It does happen, and that would be entirely your call at that time. Oh, and you are correct, we do not have a graduation or certificate of completion for any of our Clubs."

"Why is that?"

"Well, one of our Core Values is that we believe improvement never ends, and as a result, we are always learning new business and leadership strategies that we either incorporate into our curriculum or just share with our clients. Take a look at Information Technologies as an example. How fast has that changed in the past five years? Will we ever know it all? I believe not, so we develop the discipline to stay ahead as much as we can and constantly improve."

How refreshing! A Coach that practices what he preaches!

"Interesting. So my commitment to join any of your Clubs may be a lifelong commitment," I offered more as comment than a question.

Coach just looked at me with that "Is there more you want to add?" look and remained quiet.

"Coach, I just want to tell you that I am ready to join your Club should you invite me. I have learned enough about my business to know that I have many gaps that need to be filled, and you seem to know how to fill them. So we can continue with the self-assessment, or we can do the paperwork necessary to sign me up and get started." He grinned. "I also believe that you would make a good client and am excited to begin working with you, but I would like to continue and get an idea of where you are with the last two Disciplines. We may not spend as much time on each element as we have on the others, but I would like to know where you stand in all areas. Fair enough?"

Phew, I'm in!

"I just have to tell you that I am feeling a great sense of relief right now, knowing that I have someone who can really coach me to be a better CEO and train my business to have better systems. Let's get started with Information Technologies, shall we?"

And then my mounting enthusiasm was dashed as I thought of my wife. I wished she could have experienced my entire dialogue with Coach, as she may have issues with my decision to spend more money on consulting. She was *not* happy with the last decision to hire consultants and knows that money was wasted.

Well, my decision is made. I am going to have to deal with Kathy my own way.

THE SIXTH DISCIPLINE
INFORMATION
TECHNOLOGIES

*"Embrace technology,
as it is the future…"*

~ Coach ~

"I think this assessment is going to go pretty fast, as we do have a handle on our IT with very little downtime, if any. Yet I know very little about IT overall. This is one area of the business we have chosen to outsource 100%." I glanced at Coach, but couldn't get a read on what he was thinking. "We do have some of the best IT consultants in the market supporting our servers. However, I know that there are opportunities to better utilize IT for Marketing via the website. And, looking at the Core Disciplines of Business chart, I am not quite sure what this CRM thing is?"

Yeah, I am feeling really good about this Discipline.

"Okay, Ruben, tell me about your Intranet systems," he leaned back, and I imagined his legs outstretched under the desk. He looked like he was preparing for a long explanation.

"Well, not being the IT guy and not really knowing the language, I can tell you how I understand it to work. We have three different servers, one for data, one for communications (i.e. our phone system), and one to run all of the different applications we use. By design, we have our employees keep very little on their desktops; all business related files are saved on the corporate server. Employee passwords are encrypted and require to be changed every six months, and we designed an organizational chart that aligns each employee's position in the company with what data they have access to on the server."

Coach nodded, indicating that he was keeping up with me.

So far, so good!

"For example, my Accounts Receivable person can edit that field in our Accounting system, whereas my receptionist can see when clients are past due, but she does not have the authority to edit any financial data. I do get a report once a month that tells me up-time percentage, but that is about it. We are diligent about keeping our anti-virus, spy-ware, and similar applications current, and the employees are not allowed to download anything onto their desktops. In my last meeting with my IT guy, he suggested installing a new application that will restrict the types of websites our employees can access when on the web. I am still pondering that one, as it seems a bit excessive, but I am being told that is now pretty common in business."

"Wow, Ruben, you seem to have this one nailed! Great job!"

"Wow, Ruben, you seem to have this one nailed! Great job!" He leaned forward with his hand outstretched to high-five me.

This guy is cool!

"Two questions: Is all of this documented as a system? And if not, why?"

"We need to improve this overall in my company — the documentation of all these things we do well. This brings my self-assessment of Intranet to about a 3+."

"I would agree, Ruben. Now, tell me about your knowledge of Internet as a system for your business, different from the Intranet."

"Well, I would define Intranet as what we control on our computers and servers in house, and Internet is how we manage everything outside of that in the worldwide web. The only system that would apply for Internet from my perspective is access, security, and protection from being hacked or attacked, and I believe we have very strong security measures in place that limit what the employees can and cannot download. If we elect to acquire the application that limits what websites they can visit while on our system, we will be that much stronger. I cannot see what else to do here. Other than writing down our Internet security policy, I would say we have this one under control as well. I would rate us a 4 here."

I was looking at Coach's expression while I was describing our IT department and felt a bit like a kid bragging to his dad. It felt kind of good to get through two elements without much new work to be done. "So what do you say, Coach?"

"I am impressed. I cannot tell you the last time I sat down with a business owner who had so much of their IT department under control. Congratulations, Ruben, I think you will have much to contribute to the Club, especially here. Shall we move on to the next element?"

Wow, I was so focused on what I was going to get from being in Coach's Club that I never considered what I would be contributing to the other members.

I took a quick glance at the red on his big face clock and realized that we only had about fifteen minutes left.

"The next element is Website, and I believe I would give myself a 1 here. We have done nothing to maximize our website. In fact, we don't even know where to begin," I said matter- of-factly.

> *I was so focused on what I was going to get from being in Coach's Club that I never considered what I would be contributing to the other members.*

"You are not alone on that one. Can I ask you what you want your website to do?"

"What do I want it to do? I am not sure I understand the question."

"Think of the website as an employee who has a job, and that job has to be defined. Websites have one of three primary functions, or jobs: 1) to promote and generate leads/inquiries or sales, 2) to provide customer services, or 3) to be a resource for a defined community. Each purpose has a different strategy."

"I had never looked at my website that simplistically before.

Huh, Sales, Customer Service, or Resource," I said, pausing to contemplate this for a moment. "Well, I do want it to generate sales primarily. And we do have some Customer Service features and information that is important for our clients. But I do not see it as an industry resource site. So I guess it is Sales first, then Customer Service."

"Great understanding. Tell me what you would change on your home page?"

Coach had my website up on his computer, and we were looking at a rather large picture of me with the video play button in the center. Below that was information about our company history and links to credentials we hold with various agencies.

What in the world made me think a huge video of me talking about how great we are would generate leads? Man, is my ego that big?

I had to laugh out loud.

"What is so funny?" Coach asked.

"Well, there is absolutely nothing there that would cause me to want to inquire about our services. In fact, I don't even see our phone number on the home page. Wow! This has to be completely redone. Okay. Okay. Okay." I threw my hands up in the air. "I will give us a 1 on the Website element."

Actually, I was a bit embarrassed by the home page.

What in the world made me think a huge video of me talking about how great we are would generate leads? Man, is my ego that big?

"At the least, you have a direction for the site that we can coach around," he said before transitioning us into the next element, "Are you ready for CRM, Ruben?"

"I know nothing about CRM," I confessed.

"CRM stands for Contact Relationship Management. A CRM is an application a business would acquire to manage all contact relationships. Those contacts would include suspects, prospects, customers, inactive customers, vendors, strategic partners, employees, and even friends/family. Think of CRM as a database on steroids."

One of the most difficult challenges in business is adopting a new application.

"Oh, okay. We use Salesforce.com to track our leads and sales. Is that CRM?"

"Well, is your entire company using it, or just Sales?"

"Just Sales."

"Then no. A comprehensive CRM becomes the primary repository for all contact relationships companywide. Every employee who interacts with company contacts would use this one application to document meetings, conversations, tasks, problems, sales, documents, emails, and so on." Coach leaned back in his seat and stretched his arms behind his head.

"That would be nice to have. That way, we could eliminate some current redundancies we have with different databases. Okay, I am going to give myself a 1 in this area. Let's move on."

"Hold on. Tell me what would need to happen for your company to implement a CRM?"

"Sounds simple, but I can only imagine the work that would need to be done in order to fully implement a CRM (or any new application for that matter). First, we have to find the right one, customize it for our company, and teach all of the employees how to use it and make sure they are using it," I said, feeling overwhelmed with the task. "That will not be easy by any stretch of the imagination. I remember when we changed accounting software a few years back. It cost me thousands of dollars, never really worked, and after about eighteen months, we went back to QuickBooks."

"You are spot on again. One of the most difficult challenges in business is adopting a new application," he commented, glancing at the clock. "Are you ready for the last Discipline?"

"Let's do it!"

THE SEVENTH DISCIPLINE
FINANCE

*"It's not what you make that counts;
it's what you keep…"*

~ Coach ~

As I sat there reviewing my Core Disciplines of Business chart with all of its ratings, it was becoming apparent where my company had the greatest needs for improvement or, as Coach would say, "Systems, Ruben, Systems. What you can systemize, you can delegate!" Funny how it all seemed too overwhelming while I was doing the assessment, but now, looking at the chart at 30,000 feet above the trees, it seemed very logical and doable.

Somehow, somewhere during the past two meetings with Coach, I have developed a peace about this seemingly insurmountable process. I wonder how looking at the Discipline of Finance will bring me opportunities for improvement.

"Hey, Coach, why is Finance way at the end of the Disciplines?" There always seemed to be logic in everything Coach did, and I would not be at all surprised if he had a logical answer for me here.

"Great question. Someone once told me that if you are going to get into business you should get into Sales or Finance because that is where the money is made. Everything in between is getting the work completed, but without a strong hold on Sales and Finance, you can lose it all. So, when you look at the Core Disciplines you will see Growth and Finance as the two bookends."

I knew it. Either this guy is the master of making stuff up on the fly, or he really did deliberately place Growth and Finance as the bookends of the Core Disciplines. Will I ever really know?

"Finance is not my strong suit, but for some reason, I am not nervous about discussing these elements at all. It is almost as if I have personally grown over the past few meetings as a CEO. I can look back at my self-assessment and see great opportunity and strength, whereas before I was threatened by what I did not know early on in the process. Do you see that happen much?"

Every client goes through what I call the 'Executive Maturity Curve,' that guides them from the mindset of a sole proprietor to that of an effective CEO.

"I see it with every client I coach. Some faster than others, but every client goes through what I call the 'Executive Maturity Curve,' that guides them from the mindset of a sole proprietor to that of an effective CEO, but that is a talk for another day. I am proud that you are already beginning to experience that shift, as it will help you to prioritize what Disciplines and elements to address first."

"You know what else has happened? I can see where I have my people stepping all over each other. I mean, I can look down at this chart and almost look at it as if it were an organizational chart for my company. I would be the CEO responsible for the first Discipline of Culture where my managers take very structured and aligned responsibilities within the operational Disciplines." I felt like a fifty ton brick had been suddenly been lifted off of my shoulders.

"That happens quite often. Can you share with me where you see an immediate opportunity to better align some of your key people?"

"Here is an obvious one, well, obvious to me now. Under Growth, we have Sales, Marketing, Advertising, and Branding. Well, my Sales manager Bill is currently responsible for Sales, but has absolutely no input or control over our Marketing or Advertising, which we outsource. I have my Finance guy managing the Marketing vendor relationship. Now how out of whack is that? Bill should be very much involved with what the Marketing firm is doing and should be held accountable for their results, much like he is held accountable for the Sales teams results."

Man, that is so obvious now. How could I have missed that over the years? Every year, Bill asks if he could get more involved with Marketing, but I tell him he does not need the distraction from making sales. Now it is clear that they go hand in hand and need to be clearly aligned. Where the heck has my head been? I know why my wife calls me the most brilliant idiot she knows. I can hardly wait to see her face when I share that one with her, as it will bring her a healthy laugh…and I do love her laugh. I need to give her more reasons to laugh, but good reasons. I pray my marriage improves as I improve my business. God knows, she and the kids are the real reason I work so hard.

"I am feeling more confident about taking control of my future today than I have felt in a very, very, very long time. Can we get started with Finance?"

"You go ahead and get us going. You know the routine."

"Love to." I did know the routine, and I was comfortable with it. Actually, I was eager to dive right into the first element. "Budgets. I must admit that we do not do annual budgets for the company."

"Well, a company is the sum of its departments, and a true operational budget is for your departments."

"That is a completely different perspective than what I have believed a budget to be. Can you explain that a bit more?" My mind was whirling in an attempt to understand.

> *"That is a completely different perspective than what I have believed a budget to be. Can you explain that a bit more?" My mind was whirling in an attempt to understand.*

"When you think of it realistically, who spends your money in the business — you or your managers? Do you make all of the office supplies purchases? Do you purchase all of the materials needed to make your products, and do you personally manage what overtime gets approved or paid every pay period?"

"Well, no, of course not. I hired good managers to make those decisions for me."

"Now tell me how you monitor those financial decisions, if not by providing each department manager a financial plan, or a departmental budget, from which they can measure their ultimate responsibility of driving profits to your bottom line?"

His voice sounded more stern than it had all day.

"I don't. I give them full and autonomous control of my checkbook and find myself frustrated at the end of the month when we lose money." My chest was getting tighter.

Here I go again, that feeling of urgency to learn how to budget and get it in place ASAP!

"I can see from your body language that you are getting a bit anxious over this one."

Coach was right. I was getting anxious over this one because I saw it as a quick fix. "Well, of all the elements, I see this one as the fastest and most efficient way to make a huge difference in the business, immediately. Am I reading too much into this?" I really did see where I could implement this departmental budget system pretty quickly.

My boy wanted to visit LegoLand for the first time, and I promised to take him, but if I don't get a paycheck, then what can I do?

"What do you think will happen if you rush into work tomorrow and announce, with great excitement, that the company will be implementing departmental budgets immediately, and due to improper planning or understanding, it fails?" There was a cautious urgency in his voice.

Hmmm…He is reading my mind again. And I know he's right. Not too long ago, I got an idea from a friend who owns a like-sized business, and because I rushed to implement it, it failed terribly.

My managers had not fully bought into the change and were frustrated about the time and resources they had to pour into the project without first understanding what our goals were. I remember walking into the lunchroom and hearing the employees complain about all of the new policies surrounding this change and the comments by the water cooler when it did not work.

No, I don't want to repeat that experience ever again.

"Okay, Coach, I get it. At first glance, any one of these elements may appear to be quite simple to figure out, build a system, and implement, but without the proper training and coaching, there is a risk of systems failure. So, let's just say that we are at a 1 in this element and move onto the next element of Cash Flow."

It is both comforting and frustrating to sit across from Coach, knowing he has the answers I need. If only I could drain them out of his head with a huge syringe and inject them into my brain, we could be done. I want to get so many of these elements implemented NOW. I don't want to wait. Wow. I sound like a spoiled kid.

"I accept that, Ruben, but I also recognize your eagerness to get this process started. Tell me how well you have systemized a Cash Flow Analysis for your business?"

"To be totally honest, we are at a complete loss here. We don't understand why some months we make money on our P&L, but at the end of the month, we have no cash and have to tap into our line of credit to meet payroll. We always get caught up, but I would prefer to use cash to pay our bills, not a line of credit. At this point, I will have to give myself a 1 on a scale of 5 here."

"Mastering how cash flows through the business does take a deeper understanding of Finance. How often do you rely on your credit line to meet payroll or pay bills?"

"Every month. I can't seem to get ahead of it. It's very frustrating. Last month, I did not even bring home a paycheck, and my wife was not a happy camper. We had to postpone a weekend getaway that we had planned. But what do you do?"

My boy wanted to visit LegoLand for the first time, and I promised to take him, but if I don't get a paycheck, then what can I do?

"Setting up Cash Flow Analysis systems is only confusing at the beginning when determining what system works best for your company. Beyond that, it is a matter of discipline to establish some Cash Flow standards and goals, and then track them."

"What do you mean?" My mind was whirling again!

"Often something as simple as payment terms can have a tremendous impact on your Cash Flow. What are your payment terms?"

"All of our customers pay us net 30 to 45 days."

"What if 50% of those customers allowed you to hit their credit card monthly, or draft out of their checking accounts, on the 1st of each month?"

"That would be incredible! If we could get even 30% of our customers to do that, it would greatly impact our Cash Flow." He was leading me somewhere. I just didn't know exactly where.

"Is it a possibility?"

"Why, yes. In fact, we have even had new customers request that, but we don't currently offer merchant service payments or drafting services."

"Now that is just one of many possible strategies to affect how cash flows through the business. On the other side is how you manage vendor payments, or how you pay subcontractors. And so on and so on. Establishing sound Cash Flow systems requires two things: 1) having a clear understanding of all of the factors in your business that impact cash, and 2) evaluating each factor with the only goal to expedite the flow of cash to your business. Beyond that is establishing some very clear Cash Flow analysis reports that measure Cash Flow and build liquidity in the business. Do you have a liquidity target for your company?"

"No, I don't even know what that is." I braced myself.

"A sound liquidity target allows you to make financial decisions regarding use of cash. In many cases, the simple formula used is Cash on hand + AR's collectable − Trade payables = Liquidity.

The target our clients have established is six times operating overhead. This allows them the comfort of maintaining enough liquidity in the business to sustain a six-month significant downturn in the business."

"I see, but getting to that six times overhead is where we have the problem."

"I would submit to you that it is only a problem because we have not established the goal and the strategy to achieve it." The look on his face made me realize how much he wanted me to believe that I could reach any goal.

"I would submit to you that it is only a problem because we have not established the goal and the strategy to achieve it."

"You may be surprised how many different measures you will identify that will help you get there. I have seen clients move from negative liquidity to $800,000.00 liquidity in less than two years. Systems, Ruben, Systems."

"It all seems a bit farfetched while I sit in this chair, but I am sure it has been done before."

I could not even imagine what it would feel like to have a liquidity of $800,000.00. *Total fantasy, at this point, to me.* For the first time, I felt like Coach was fighting me on an issue. I felt it strange and wanted to ask him.

"For the first time, I felt like you were pushing me to see something your way. In no other encounter have I felt that way. What changed?"

"I did push you," he smiled. "It is important for me to see how you react when pushed, and you did fine." Yet another deliberate move on Coach's agenda.

Can this really be true for everything he does?

"Let's get beyond Cash Flow and move to Capital and Debt Services. What can you tell me about that?"

"Other than the line of credit, we have not had to borrow any money, so I feel pretty good about our position here. I would give us a 4+."

"Very nice, Ruben, but if I were to look at your balance sheet, how much debt would I see there?"

"Well, there is the loan I made to the company, some deferred income to me, and a small amount on credit cards, and one piece of machinery that has not fully depreciated. I can tell you that one of the reasons we struggle with Cash Flow is because we pay our bills and buy very little on credit. I strongly believe in funding your own growth versus having to depend on a third party to get us there." I wanted him to know how serious I was about this.

"Great philosophy to have, and obviously, it has served you well. I also share your philosophy on debt and use of Capital, but you may have to establish guidelines for others to follow that are consistent with that philosophy. Those guidelines would constitute the established systems for the company regarding this element." He glanced at the clock. "For example, we will not increase our administrative or management cost unless we can justify it against our liquidity position. That applies to every manager in the company, including myself. Now tell me, how would a policy like that help you as the CEO?"

"Well, it would certainly make it clear to all of my managers when we are in a financial position to increase administrative or management payroll. It could also create a bit of competitiveness for those monies once they become available. That could be a good thing. It would tell me the managers are really watching their dollars. Would this be true for asset purchases as well?"

"Why don't you try to answer that?"

I should have known I would be answering my own question — again!

"Well, I guess it would. Regardless if the cost is payroll, or ongoing, or a purchase which is one time, the question to answer is: Can we afford it and use liquidity, or some other like indicator?"

"You are getting it! So, prior to this conversation, how have you made payroll decisions?"

"By the seat of our pants. We get busy and hire people, only to be faced with the reality of having to let them go when volume stops or is greatly reduced."

I have hated every lay-off.

The worst was the young lady who was so good, but we just didn't have the work for her. She cried and pled for her job, and I felt nothing but anger with myself…like somehow, I knew that it was something I had done or not done that was forcing this talented girl to lose her job and crumble in front of me. It was terrible, and there was nothing I could do. We were bleeding cash, and it was all labor in her department. I went home that evening and told my wife about the experience, only to hear an "I told you so." She had gotten mad at me for hiring her in the first place, believing that we could have gotten that department productive with better-managed overtime and cross-training underutilized employees from other departments. In that case, she was correct, and I should have listened to her. But at the end of the day, if I had some established guidelines for making those decisions, I would not have been in that position at all.

I have hated every lay-off.

"I have probably lost hundreds of thousands of dollars by making such decisions without any guidelines. Do you have any idea how a strong system here would help us to make better big ticket purchasing ideas? Add that to each department manager having a monthly budget they report to and strong Cash Flow systems. We can get our liquidity up relatively fast. I am beginning to see it." It had happened again. I came into this Discipline thinking that each element functioned independent of each other, but in reality, they all touch each other, and when well-systematized, they greatly strengthen the unit.

It is so clear now, when ten minutes ago, I thought I was in an argument with Coach. How does he do that?

"Ruben, as you fully learn, appreciate, implement, and trust the Core Disciplines of Business and its systems, you will see not only how the elements within a Discipline support each other, but you will see an amazing matrix where all twenty-seven elements support and interact with each other. But that will come in time." He again glanced at the clock, and I knew we were about to run out of time.

"I believe that. As for Capital and Debt Service, I have to give us another 1 out of 5 because we currently have no guidelines or systems in place here. Although I think we are doing well by not carrying a lot of debt, we have wasted hundreds of thousands of dollars by not having a good system for this. I am okay with that."

"Then let's wrap it up with KPI's. What do you know about Key Performance Indicators?"

"Very little, to be truthful with you. What are they?" I was beginning to feel upset. I had so much information swirling around my mind.

"When you go to the doctor, they almost always take some basic readings with every visit. Can you tell me what those readings are?"

"It has been a very long time since I was last at the doctor, but I will try to remember."

Another thing my wife has been on me about. I really do need to get my six-month checkup back on my calendar.

"Let's see, the nurse takes your weight, blood pressure, temperature, oxygen level, and possibly asks you a few questions about having any pain or recently developed discomfort. Is that about it?"

"I think you got it. Now, what do you think the doctor does with that information?"

"Probably not much, unless blood pressure or other numbers are way off. The rest of the information is only useful if the situation is extreme."

"You are probably right. So why take the time and pay a nurse to gather that information with every visit?"

"I guess they are important to keep and track for historical reasons." I started to see where Coach was going with this.

"You are getting close. You see, KPI's really tell you nothing by themselves. But when compared to a history of consistent measuring, or when charted against established baselines, what begins to happen?"

"Well, we can see more clearly if we are way off in one area or another."

"Correct, will that awareness tell the doctor exactly what action to take?" He pushed me to think about this on a deeper level.

KPI's are indicators and nothing more.

"Well, no, he/she would have to dig a lot deeper to understand the problem before taking any action."

"You got it. You see, KPI's are *indicators* and nothing more. They require that you understand them, know how to compare them, and are astute enough to interpret them when needed. Your action will be the result of the interpretation and investigation, not the KPI's themselves. However, if you track the correct KPI's, you will be kept abreast of the pulse of your business." Coach's voice held the familiar passion. I could tell he really loved his work.

"How do you determine what are the best KPI's to track?"

"Now *that* is the magic question. Every CEO and every department manager should have 3-7 KPI's they measure regularly in order to be kept abreast of the overall company performance, and these KPI's may shift from time to time if needed. So, here is a simple example. The department manager may have a production KPI of $500,000 in a thirty backlog at all times (backlog meaning the dollar value of new orders waiting to enter production). The CEO may have determined that number based on what needs to ship monthly in order to invoice enough to exceed monthly expenses. Now, Monday morning comes around and backlog falls to $100,000. What happens?"

"Well, the CEO would have to go and find out why it fell off by so much and so fast. It could be that shipping got way ahead and was able to put the work out faster and as a result exhausted the backlog. Or, it could be that the Sales department had an order that was in the backlog figures and was pulled back by the customer, or there can be other factors at play here. We really do not know."

"And what happens if we ignore it?" He asked, with a twinkle in his eye.

"That would be dumb. If that were a true scenario, the CEO would have to act quickly by having his Production manager rapidly reschedule work to cut labor hours, and he would have to meet with the Sales manager to evaluate what is in the pipeline for sales in the upcoming thirty days. They may even have to offer incentives to customers to place orders quickly. But you cannot just ignore that reality," I answered confidently.

"Right answer, but here is the deeper question. What happens to the CEO who has no KPI's and, as a result, has no visibility of this pending crisis?"

Oh my God! Coach had just hit me right between the eyes, as this had recently happened to me. It was one week before Thanksgiving when I was told we did not have enough in shipping to invoice and, as a result, we were going to send employees home for the entire Thanksgiving week without pay. Although they all received a frozen Turkey, they were not happy with me. One of our key customers lost one of their top customers, and in the process, had to cancel a sizable order we were geared up to run that week. In fact, that was the only job we had that week. I remember asking myself, *How could this happen? How could I have been caught so off guard that we had to send our team home for one week without pay?*

I winced. "Yeah, I can see the power of KPI's at all levels in the business."

"Ruben, here is a very important CEO Rule to remember, 'People respond to what they measure.' And in the event that they are not measuring KPI's, what are they responding to?"

People respond to what they measure.

Hmmm…people respond to what they measure. Now that makes total sense. We have to get these KPI's going, along with everything else.

"Coach, if all of my managers had KPI's for their departments, it would change their lives. I mean *really* change their ability to assess their departments objectively, and they would have very clear guidelines. My God, this one is HUGE."

"You are really getting the essence of the Core Disciplines, Ruben. I could not have said it any better. Remember, numbers never lie, people do…often to themselves."

Yeah, I know that is true. I had convinced myself that I knew how to run a business before I met this guy.

I took a glance at the clock on Coach's desk. We had exactly five minutes left, and we were done with the self-assessment. Somehow, Coach got it all done with time to spare.

"Well, I believe you are done. How do you feel?" He flashed a comforting smile.

"I am a mixed bag of emotions. I am excited, anxious to get started, and a bit fearful of all the change we are going to face as we shift to a systems company," I confessed.

"I can appreciate that. Thank you for honestly answering my question. Now, what do you want to do next?" He inquired once again, as if he had never heard me say I was ready to join his Club.

I guess he really wants to know I'm committed.

"I want to join your CEO Club. How can we get started?"

Coach reached in his drawer and pulled out what looked like an enrollment agreement. He turned it towards me and then asked me one final question: "Ruben, if you fill out this paperwork to join, and we schedule our first Coaching Session, and you attend your first CEO Club next week…What would cause you to say next week that you could not go forward?" The tone in his voice was very serious.

I guess he really does want to make sure I'm in 100%.

"Coach, I am a man of my word. If I join, I am all in."

Just as I finished my declaration, I could hear my wife's voice: *You spent how much for a business coach?*

"Well, there may be one thing. You see, Coach, my wife may not be too happy about this decision. That is not to say that she will stop it, but she sure can make it hard for me."

"Thank you for our honesty, Ruben. Let's do this. I will take the paperwork back, and let's schedule another meeting where you will walk through that door, look me in the eyes, and say that it is not the right time to join, or you will give me a check for the down payment, we will complete this paperwork, and get you started in the program. Fair enough?"

"Yes, that is very fair. When do you want to meet?"

We compared calendars, set an appointment for the following week, and I was free of anxiety thinking that I had just made a key decision without Kathy's input.

What a classy move on Coach's end...

I had to ask. "You could have easily gotten your deposit check today and the signed agreement. Why did you not let me do that? I thought in sales, you close when the deal is hot, and I am hot and ready."

"Two reasons, Ruben. One is that I have never had to sell anyone on joining our CEO Club. Every member is in that class for their reasons, not mine. And secondly, I believe that my clients, when they joined, came to me with eyes wide open, free of the thought or doubt of having made a poor decision. Your wife's probable objections are a source of doubt, no matter how hot and ready you are."

Again, my mind began to wonder about my current Sales team, and what we could produce if we had half the Sales strategies Coach demonstrated. I don't have one Sales representative who would have done what Coach just did. No, they, including myself, would have walked out of this office with a check and signed paperwork.

I really do have much to learn from Coach, in so many different areas.

Coach stood up, grabbed his coat and briefcase, and walked me out to the parking lot since he was on his way home.

I got a hug from Coach and renewed my promise to see him next week.

As I was driving home, my mind kept thinking of all the elements, how they interact, and how, when systemized, they can greatly strengthen a unit. The seemingly easy ones like a Customer Feedback system to the more difficult Finance elements.

Each one is filled with opportunity and excitement. And when I look at the Core Disciplines of Business as a business model and road map for eliminating gaps, I also see how it can clearly align our people, especially our leaders. I can see how we will all be on the same page with a clear understanding of our roles and responsibilities.

I took a quick glance at my speedometer (a dashboard KPI?) and had to slow down from 90 m.p.h. I had not even realized that I was speeding.

Wow, imagine where my company can be in two short years if we embrace the philosophy of business systems and follow the Core Disciplines of Business to get there. There are no limits.

I arrived home early for the first time in who knows how long. My 8-year-old son was out riding his bike and gave me one of those head nods when he rode by.

I remember when he would scream with excitement when I opened the front door.

How things can change so fast when your priorities are all mixed up. Another outcome I am expecting from this investment is a balanced life — a life like Coach's where my day can end at 5 p.m. predictably with half-day Fridays.

I remember when he would scream with excitement when I opened the front door. How things can change so fast when your priorities are all mixed up. Another outcome I am expecting from this investment is a balanced life — a life like Coach's where my day can end at 5 p.m. predictably with half-day Fridays.

I chuckled to myself.

Coach has enlightened me much in just two meetings, but the real and only proof is in the results.

FOUR YEARS LATER

"Ruben, you are the one who saved your business and your family. And you are the one who will save your life."

~ Coach ~

Come on, Coach. Don't be busy. Pick up the phone. I need to talk with you.

When he picked up, I finally inhaled. "Hey, Coach."

"Ruben! So glad to hear from you! How are you?" His voice immediately calmed me down.

"Well, Coach, that's what I'm calling you about. I got some bad news today."

"What's that, Ruben? Is it something I can help you with?" The concern in his voice was genuine, and for a moment, I flashed back on all of the pivotal moments in the last four years.

I had joined the Club, with only a bit of static from my wife. But it wasn't long before she realized that this was the best investment I had ever made — not just for the business, but for us.

> *"I found out today that I have cancer."*

Coach gave me my life back.

"Ruben?" His concerned voice brought me back to the present.

"Yeah, Coach. Sorry. Yeah, uh, I don't know how to say this…" My voice and thoughts started to trail off again. "I found out today that I have cancer."

After a brief pause, Coach responded. "Ruben, I'm sorry to hear that." And then, in true Coach style, he went where he always did, "What's your plan for eliminating the cancer?"

I laughed out loud, and he laughed with me, the same way he had so many times before.

"Well. I meet with a doctor Monday to talk treatment. They say I only have six months, but I'm thinking *they don't know what they don't know.*"

"Yes, and what they don't know is who this cancer is playing with. I've never met anyone with as much tenacity and drive. If anyone can kick this beast to the curb, it's you, Ruben. Now, how can I be of service to you?"

—*∿∿*—

If I had been diagnosed four years ago, I would have lost everything.

—*∿∿*—

"Well, in order to put the time and energy into the treatment, I need to step away from the business for a while. Can we review the succession plan? I'd like to have this ready by Monday as well."

"Absolutely. I have time right now. Let's do it."

It took us only one hour to review the plan, make some minor adjustments, and strategize the next move. We were tying up the call when I felt overcome with emotion.

"Coach…" I started, but didn't know how to put my feelings into words.

"Yes, Ruben? Did we miss something?"

"No, we haven't missed anything. I just need to say Thank You. I know I've said it many times before, but this time, it's even more important to me that you hear it. If I had been diagnosed four years ago, I would have lost everything. The anxiety that I feel now, I know, is nothing close to what I would have been experiencing then. There is no way I could have imagined walking away from the business for even a week, let alone months. But because of you and your support in helping me to implement the Core Disciplines of Business, I can take the time I need to do this." I took a deep breath. "Coach, you didn't just save my business and my family. You have given me the chance to save my own life. How could I ever thank you?" I pushed down the lump in my throat to get through it, but the tears brimmed my eyes.

"Ruben, *you* are the one who saved your business and your family. And *you* are the one who will save your life. And you're welcome. It's been an absolute pleasure to coach you and witness your growth — as a businessman, a leader, a family man, and a mentor. I am here in whatever capacity you need me."

"Thank you, Coach."

"You're welcome. Now, you have a plan to execute. Call me if you have any questions between now and Monday, and please keep me updated."

"You got it. We're leaving for a little family getaway, but I'll contact you Monday."

I sat back in my big leather chair and closed my eyes.

He's right. I am going to kick this thing's butt. I do have what it takes. I'm only forty-nine years old, and in four years, with his coaching, I have saved my business and my family.

When I met him, my business was bleeding cash. My top leaders and experienced employees were quitting. Customers were quitting, too, and I had no idea how to get my arms around it.

In the CEO Club meetings, we had dealt with the toughest issues in our businesses. I had no idea how much I could learn from a room full of non-competing CEO's. Their wisdom, experiences, insight, resources, and best practices have saved me hundreds of thousands of dollars. We have laughed together, argued together, negotiated best practices together, and, yes, on occasion, shed a tear or two as we matured over the years.

Today, 100% of the systems are designed, implemented, monitored, and audited by the team, and what an incredible difference it has made. The business now generates over $10,000,000.00 in revenues, has sixty-two employees, and can boast that its GP is 47% with a 13% net before taxes, its liquidity is twelve times monthly operating expenses, and it has no debt after only eight years in operation. Today, I am freer as a CEO than I have ever been.

But his impact has reached beyond the walls of my business.

Coach and his family had become part of our family, as had many members of my CEO Club. We traveled together, attended our kids' sporting events together, shared many meals together and, most importantly, become special friends.

My relationship with my family now resembled Coach's. I regularly left work at 5:00 p.m. and enjoyed half-day Fridays. I rarely went into the office on the weekends, and my family life had improved tremendously. My wife was no longer concerned or involved in the business at all. We had date night every Friday and tried to take a minimum of three family vacations and three long weekend getaways per year.

My life changed the day I met Coach, and I thank God for that.

"Honey?" Kathy's voice brought me back into the office.

"Yes?"

"We need to get to the airport. Our plane leaves in three hours."

"Let's go!" I smiled and jumped out of the chair to give her a hug.

Three hours later, I was sitting on a plane headed to Florida, with my wife and son, for a much-needed getaway.

"Hi, my name is Bill." The young man sitting next to me was dressed well but looked a bit frazzled as he introduced himself.

"Hi, Bill."

"Can I ask you what you mean by that statement you wrote down on your notepad?"

I looked down at the very first words Coach wrote years ago, "Begin with the end in mind."

"Sure, but can I ask you a question first?"

"Yeah." He beamed with curiosity.

I kind of liked this young man's spunk.

"Do you own a business?"

"As a matter of fact, I do, but can I get your name?"

"Yes. My friends call me Coach."

Whether I have six months, six years, or a few decades left, I plan on making an impact.

DO YOU KNOW
YOUR NEXT MOVE?

ESTRADA STRATEGIES

YOUR NEXT MOVE

You have a deeper understanding of The 7 Core Disciplines of Business, but...

> Do you know which of the Disciplines or
> elements to implement first?

> Are you certain that you know how to implement that change
> seamlessly — without putting yourself in "checkmate"?

Implementing The 7 Core Disciplines of Business is, as you saw in the story, quite a task. It can take up to two years with the support of a CEO Coach at Estrada Strategies. who understands all of the subtleties of the Disciplines.

At Estrada Strategies. we are committed to providing the world-class training, coaching, and monitoring you need to identify your next move and make it powerfully, so that you can enjoy phenomenal growth in your business and the freedom you desire to live your best life.

Reach out to a CEO Coach at Estrada Strategies
for a FREE Consultation today.
Visit us at www.EstradaStrategies.com/Ontario
or Contact Us By Phone:
1.800.ESTRADA

ABOUT RUBEN

Ruben A. Estrada was the CEO and chief small business architect of Estrada Strategies, LLC, and founder of the CEO Club™, Entrepreneurs Club, and the monthly Executive On-Line CLUB and Business Coaching systems.

In 2000, Ruben formed Estrada Strategies, LLC with the Vision of helping all businesses succeed. In 2005 he expanded the reach of that vision by creating Estrada Strategies Franchise Inc. and launching the first franchise operation in Knoxville, TN. In 2012, with a team of seven associates serving over 500 clients, Estrada Strategies provides services that include business systems training including sales systems, executive leadership development, systems management, organization development, strategic planning, financial management, and much more. Using a behavior modification model that integrates training, coaching, and monitoring ensures that Estrada Strategies' clients realize significant improvements in revenues and profits. Today, ES serves clients across the United States from offices in southern California, Tennessee and Colorado. The company continues to expand with plans to launch offices in up to 20 new locations.

Ruben's expertise for rebuilding existing companies and for establishing new operations made him a leader among entrepreneurs and CEOs of small businesses. His ability to develop and implement new market penetration and acquisition plans gave his clients the edge in growing their businesses. Using the "Core Disciplines of Business™", Ruben helped many entrepreneurs realize their full potential. His many clients have realized significant increases in revenues, gross profits, and net income. They have also learned how to develop and implement systems to improve performance throughout their companies. The partners who shared his early vision and the coaches they trained at Estrada Strategies continue this work.

Prior to launching Estrada Strategies, Ruben worked 16 years with a now publicly held company. In the last ten years of his corporate career, Ruben opened new operations for the corporation in a series of West coast cities. Over that 10-year period, Ruben grew the new operations to beyond $21 million in annual revenues and won numerous awards and recognition for service excellence and unprecedented growth.

In 2004, Ruben created the Estrada Strategies Foundation to serve those small businesses that were not in a financial position to invest in an Estrada Strategies business coaching program. The Foundation is now recognized as Inland Southern California's Small Business Resource Liaison serving start-ups, and youth in high school/college aspiring to be entrepreneurs in addition to struggling small business owners.

An internationally recognized keynote speaker and an Inland Empire community leader, Ruben Estrada served on several corporate and community boards and was the recipient of numerous business and community awards. A deeply spiritual and family man, he lived in San Bernardino, California with his wife Lori, daughter Brittany, and son Ruben Jr. until he passed in November, 2012.

Beyond the impact he had on businesses and the economy, Ruben's true impact can hardly be measured with words. He was a beloved husband and father, and a life-changing mentor to many.

"Who was Ruben before cancer, and who is Ruben after cancer? Before cancer, I was always looking for more hours in the day, more days in the week, and more weeks in the month to get all my work done. Today is a different story. You see, while I was 'making arrangements,' and choosing to live through the war against cancer, I knew there was a reason I was allowed to survive. That reason was revealed to me, and it was made crystal clear what impact I was supposed to make on this world; and should I survive, everything I do must align with that purpose, or Impact. ALL MY LIFE, I WAS FOCUSING ON THE WRONG END OF THE SPECTRUM. All my life, I asked for more time, 'Please give me more Capacity,' when the solution was not more hours in a day. No, the solution was a shift of focus from Capacity to Impact. You see, now that I am clear on the Impact and focus only on that Impact, my Capacity has quadrupled. I cannot tell you exactly how; there is no recipe for this…only a shift of focus. If you want to do more, stop trying to do more and focus on Impact. 'So, Ruben, give me an example of impact,' you might say. That, my friendly reader, is a story for another day."

ACKNOWLEDGMENTS

First, I thank God, for bringing me the knowledge and discipline to write this book.

Thank you to the hundreds of people who encouraged and pestered me when needed ("Where are you with the book?" Man, how I hated that question!) to keep writing over the past few years.

Thank you, Lori, for taking the time to read every word I wrote and offer the sound "common sense" feedback one can only get from their spouse of more than 24 years. No one knows me better. I love you.

Thank you to my children Brittany and Ruben Jr., who along with your mother, are the reason I shifted my focus in life. You inspired me to work hard to impact your lives, so that you can have an impact on others!

Thank you, Bruce Seidman, for your mentorship and guidance. You're the best.

And, finally, thank you to Amanda Johnson and the True Intention team for your expertise during the final phases of editing and publishing this book.

CPSIA information can be obtained
at www.ICGtesting.com
Printed in the USA
FSHW021252270319
56730FS